I0450329

The Selected Works of Bela Kun
First Prism Key Press Edition 2011

Prism Key Press
New York, NY 10001
PrismKeyPress.com

ISBN-13: 978-1468092585

The Selected Works of Bela Kun

CONTENTS

A Disciplined and Centralised Leadership

The time has not yet come to write the history of the five years of the Russian revolution, and even if it had, it would not be the task of the Fourth World Congress to write that history, although it has been a first rank and file participator in the making of that history. All the more reason for us, therefore, to carefully and discriminately collect all the experiences of the Russian Revolution and to take judicious views of these experiences in our revolutionary struggle. All of us who have fought in the Russian revolution and have led in revolutionary fights outside of Russia have built up some more or less faulty generalized theories. Almost none of us has avoided these errors. We ought to avoid Utopianism of every kind, applying our experiences with the utmost discrimination in regard to West European conditions. We ought to endeavour to inaugurate, on the basis of the experiences of the Russian revolution, a similarly realist revolutionary policy in the West, as the policy of the Russian Communist Party has always been and continues to be.

It is now my task to point out the subjective factor of the proletarian revolution, to describe the role of the Russian Communist Party in the proletarian revolution, even if only in fragmentary outline. Permit me in this connection to draw a parallel between the great Russian revolution and the abortive Hungarian revolution. On looking back at the history of these five years we have to confess that a miracle has happened.

The power of the Soviets is alive and strong to-day in spite of the offensive of the now defunct German imperialism, the united offensive of the capitalists of all countries, and the vicious activities of Russian and the international Mensheviki. The invincibility of the Russian revolution, of the Russian Soviets, is due to factors, the absence of which in Hungary was the cause of the collapse of the Hungarian proletarian dictatorship.

I do not intend to enlarge upon the international and internal political causes which were favourable to the Russian revolution, and which, on the other hand, were detrimental to the Hungarian revolution. I shall only point to the fact that in Hungary we failed to provide, not only what Comrade Lenin described as a plan of retreat, but even a line of retreat. In regard to the Russian revolution, I think that the circumstance which has belied all the Thermidor prophesies about Soviet Russia was the following:—In Russia there was a centralized, disciplined and self-sacrificing Workers' Pary in the shape of the Russian Communist Party. The absence of such a Party or of anything approaching it in Hungary was the cause of the inevitable collapse of the proletarian revolution, notwithstanding all the sacrifices and enthusiasm of the Hungarian proletariat and poorer peasantry. Apart from military defeat at the front, the downfall of the revolution was accelerated by the vacillating influence of the social democracy upon the Hungarian working class. The Russian proletariat and its glorious Red Army at that time and afterwards sustained a number of defeats on the various counter-revolutionary fronts. There were moments in Russia when, in the midst of great dangers, the Russian working class began to waver. There were times when the state of mind of a section of the working class was, if not positively, at least passively, counter-revolutionary. There were times when the wavering, starving and tired working class gave to the superficial observer sufficient reason for prophesying a Thermidor to Soviet Russia. It is enough to recall the period of the Kronstadt mutiny. Yet all the effects of these waverings of a part of the working class were neutralized.

We, in Hungary, did not have the benefit of a mature Communist Party, and I am safe in saying that at the time we could not have such a Party. We had no mature Communist Party that could cling to the helm of State at the most critical moments, in spite of the wavering of the working class, in spite of the passive, and at times even hostile, attitude of part of the

8

working class. In Hungary influence was brought to bear upon the masses of the proletariat by the fusion between the class-conscious active and determined minoritv and the social democracy, which, together, led the masses to the conquest of power. On the other hand, in Russia there has been, and there is now, a Communist Party with years of fighting experience, whose influence in the critical moments of the Russian revolution was enormous. This party, whose class character stands out in prominent relief during these last five years of revolution, has become the party of the Russian people. The German Social Democratic Party, at the Goerlitz Conference, finally discarded its class mask, declaring itself the "Volkspartei" (People's Party), instead of the greatest class party in the world, which it was as the German Social-Democratic Party. It is now really the party of the petty bourgeoisie, and, as such, it has become the servant of the big bourgeoisie of Germany. As against this, the Russian Communist Party, having strictly maintained its class character during the entire period of the dictatorship, has truly become the party of all the toiling elements of the Russian people. This will not be believed in social democratic circles, and there are even communists who doubt it. But I will quote just one instance which will suffice to show that the Russian Communist Pary is really the party of the Russian people ands that every Communist is, so to speak, the spokesman of the toiling elements of the Russian people. Last year we had a party cleaning of the Russian Party of elements that were undesirable. This cleaning was conducted at public meetings of non-party workers, in the presence of the entire mass of the unattached factory workers. Every non-party worker and every non-party peasant had the opportunity to object to any member remaining in the Communist Party, and the non-party workers and peasants made full use of this right. To be a Communist in Russia—let me repeat it once more—is to be the spokesman of the people. This makes the Communist Party in Russia a real party of the toiling people, although it has strictly maintained its proletarian character throughout the five years of the revolution.

9

This is the real reason of the wonderful development of the Party. It rests, naturally, in its revolutionary policy and in its wonderful flexible tactics. Nevertheless, we must ask whence did the Party obtain such a policy and such an influence over the working class. What is it that enabled the Russian Party not only to gain a majority at the time of the October revolution, but to retain it throughout the vicissitudes of the revolution? The secret lies first of all in the close organization of the Party. No other party, bourgeois or proletarian, had such a carefully picked and strongly welded nucleus, or to, use a favourite military metaphor of Comrade Bukharin, a uniform ideological general staff, as has the Russian Party.

This party, this General Staff, this nucleus, this fundamental group, was built up during the long years of struggle. During these struggles the opportunist elements were swept out of the Party, not only mechanically, but also by deliberate elimination. All elements that were unsuitable to the close circle of fighters were weeded out of the ranks. On the other hand, the Russian Communist Party, in the course of its struggles, not only developed its nucleus, but also brought new elements into the movement which became welded to the nucleus. It has become a party really capable of organizing and leading the masses, not hangers-on, not intellectuals who refuse to submit to art disci line, but real workers. The characteristic feature of the five years of the Russian revolution was that all the Menshevik and Social Revolutionary elements who were really faithful to the workers and to the working class were gradually absorbed by the Russian Communist Party. There was nothing left in the Menshevist and Social Revolutionary Parties but a few intellectual scribes who had nothing whatever to do with the Labour movement; who were, so to speak, guests, and not leaders of the working class. The influence of the Communist Party over the large working class masses, with the State under Communist control, is naturally exercised not only by means of propaganda, but also by the authority of the State and of the administration

In this way, wherever workers go, wherever workers are occupied, you can meet a Bolshevik, a Communist. The Soviet institutions, the Soviet administration offices, may be as faulty as Comrade Lenin has said they are. Nevertheless, thanks to the Communist Party, they have become a kind of proletarian democracies. The Soviet organs, through the Communist Party, have become the organs of proletarian democracy, and not vice-versa. A comparison with the history of the Hungarian Soviets will show this clearly. In Hungary we have had Soviets —such Soviets as Gorter or the German Independents would have them —but without Communist leadership. The organs elected by the suffrage of the large masses of the proletariat did not really become the organs of the working class. They were not the expression of the will of the proletariat. Here, in Russia, where the Mensheviks demanded free election to the Soviets, where all reformist elements from Martov to Miliukov united for free Soviet elections against the Bolshevik dictatorship, the Soviet organs are much more the organs of the proletarian democracy than the freely elected ones of Hungary which were not led by Communists.

In Hungary there was no united Communist leadership of the Soviets and the Trade Unions. The Trade Unions claimed the leadership of the State because they were much more proletarian than the Soviets, which contained non-proletarian elements. It was a struggle between the Soviets and the Trade Unions, and the Trade Unions could claim with right that they represented to a greater extent than the Soviets the opinions of the large masses and the class character of the proletariat. There resulted a conflict between the reformistic, social-democratic Trade Union leaders and the Soviets. The workers went more willingly into the Trade Unions, which were led by Labour leaders, even though reformists, than into the Soviets, where no Communist leadership existed. In Russia, with the help of the Communist Party, the Soviets became a real popular institution, an organ of proletarian democracy. In Hungary we could not achieve this because there was no Communist leadership. But how is it possible to achieve united action in such a large country with so many State organs, with so many labour organizations? How is it possible, in a country where there are single districts much larger than France, Germany and England together, to find a unified party leadership which could be felt even in the smallest village?

How is centralization at all possible in such a country as Russia? I would like to answer this question by a comparison. In Germany the social-democracy, having attained power, was practically dissolved as a party organization. The governmental organs influenced the social democracy much more than the latter influenced the government. The deciding factor in the social-democracy is the governmental social-democratic bureaucracy which originated from the old party bureaucracy. If is just the opposite in Russia. The Russian Party always saw to it that the leading elements of the Party should influence the Soviet organs, and not vice-versa. To bring this about something was required from the Communist Party which is still not understood by many persons otherwise well acquainted with the Russian movement. This is what I said yesterday to one of the comrades of our Party: Russia is not a Prussian sergeant, and we are not recruits. Moscow represents the best leadership of the world revolution. Those who do not understand the significance of centralized discipline as the experience of the Russian Revolution created it are not good recruits of Communism or of the Communist Party. The leadership of the whole State apparatus by the Communist Party in a country as vast as Russia is a most difficult task. The history of the last five years shows that the forces of the Party are to be totally regrouped to meet the new task which the revolution put before the Party. Such a weapon as the New Economic Policy could not possibly be applied without a strict discipline in the Communist Party. It was only by a radical regrouping of the forces of our Party that we were able to carry out this policy without any great crisis in our Party.

How can we explain this discipline? Of course, there is

the story that old-time Bolsheviks were an organization of conspirators under the leadership of Comrade Lenin. I am sorry to say that I was not a party to such conspiracy, and do not know what sort of conspirators they were. I know, however, that these conspirators have become the best leaders of the masses. Why? Because during this conspiring period of the Russian revolution a strict discipline was created and the members of the Party were trained in this discipline. Naturally, this discipline comes not only from the masses, but mainly from the leaders, and it requires therefore a great confidence in the leaders. This leadership is really the heart of the Russian Communist Party, the authoritative body of the whole Communist movement. Allow me to quote these few words from the Austrian poet Anzengruber: —*"Thou shalt honour thy father and thy mother, but they must be worthy of it."* The leaders of the Russian Revolution have gained the confidence of the masses and of the Communist Party because they have been worthy of it.

The iron discipline of the Russian Communist Party was what made it possible to carry on their elastic policy. I do not intend to say why this policy is elastic. The cause and source of the elasticity is well known to all. There is no body in the world where Marxism has been so completely incorporated as in the Communist Party of Russia; but the best Marxian analysis remains only an historical document when there is no organization sufficiently elastic to act in accordance with this analysis. Without a strict discipline, without well-organized cadres, the accomplishment of such a policy would be impassible. At the present time, in the sixth year of the revolution, the Communist Party of Russia is being faced with its greatest problem since the beginning of the revolution. It is, how to apply the Economic Policy under the leadership of a working class political party so that the realization of this policy might not bring into the Party certain petty bourgeois elements. The Communist Party of Russia has stood the test, thanks to its discipline and its elastic organization. Centralization and centralised discipline are the greatest lessons which we have been able to learn in the Russian Communist Party. Some of the best theses of the Comintern, it seems to me, are those of the Second Congress on the rule of the Communist Party in the proletarian revolution. These theses have had the same effect, on a less intense scale, than the Communist Party of Russia has had in the Russian revolution. The activity of the Communist Party of Russia should be a subject of study for every leader and organizer of the Western parties so that they may make critical use of the Russian experience in the Western situation and prepare their parties for the conquest and maintenance of power. The application of this experience is not the least problem of the International Revolution.

I am far from being an adherent of the free will doctrine, but I believe that for a realization of the prospects of a world revolution, the subjective factor of a Communist Party is one of the most important. We cannot determine the objective factors, at most we can influence them through the Communist Party. Nevertheless, I believe that if we had had Communist parties like the Russian one in 1919 in every country, at the time of the demobilization crisis, we would have been able not only to seize power, but also to have held it. The importance of the Communist Party as a subjective factor remains the same even in this period of comparative apathy. The question before us is: Considering the prospects for a world revolution, how can we build up such Communist parties which, in Western circumstances, perhaps through different means, can gradually win over the majority of the proletariat, before the revolution and after the revolution? Is it possible to create such Communist parties? I believe so. I have been working within the Communist Party of Russia, and I can say that the masses of its membership do not stand on a higher intellectual level than the German proletariat. I might even say that the masses of the German proletariat stand higher in culture than those of the Russian Communist Party. Of course, behind the Russian proletariat are five long years of experience in revolution; it is this experience which has made possible the elastic policy of the Russian Party.

But such elasticity is possible in all parties. I believe that the main problem in building up such subjective factors of the world revolution is the creation of basic revolutionary cadres. I believe that if we are able to form these cadres, these vanguard troops, we will be able to lead the Western proletariat to the conquest of power, and retain this power after we have gained it. That is why this is one of our chief tasks, and the lessons which the Russian Communist Party has given us from five years of experience in the Russian revolution are most important.

A New Centre of Infection

Not long ago Count Czernin, the former Austrian Minister for Foreign Affairs, was formally repudiating territorial annexations at the expense of the Russian Revolution. At that time the disturbances in the Austro-Hungarian monarchy were only beginning. The frightened ruling classes of the Danubian monarchy were then still having recourse to methods which were successful, up to a certain point, in disguising the dissolution of capitalism.

Since that time, however, Austria-Hungary also has become a nest of revolutionary infection. The German Imperialists are now not only imposing their quarantine on the Russian frontier: they are defending themselves against the revolutionary bacilli drifting in from amongst the peoples of Austria-Hungary.

The note of the German Government demands the isolation of German prisoners of war, not only from Russian Soviet agents, but also from the "allied" Austrian and Hungarian prisoners. In the eyes of the German Government, the subjects of the Hapsburg Monarchy now in Russia are one mass of "infection." The German Imperialists have become aware of a new danger — a danger arising from an "allied" country, and portending revolution nearer home. The revolts in Austria-Hungary are now not problems of the future, but questions of the day; they are not isolated hunger riots that blaze up, here and there, but harbingers of revolution, steadily making their appearance in all corners of the monarchy.

The ground has been splendidly prepared for revolution, despite the fact that the official Social-Democratic Party has completely abstained from taking part in these risings. Germany is daily making new impossible demands on Austria-Hungary; the broken Monarchy cannot satisfy these demands; and the German Imperialists are treating it in exactly the same way as the "great" Powers before the war treated Turkey.

The reins of power in Hungary are once again in the hands of Tisza, that best disciple of the Ministers of Tsarism, hated by the whole of Hungary. Even in 1912 he drew up a row of machine guns in front of the Hungarian Parliament, and bombarded the demonstrating workers with artillery. Tisza is the last hope of the Monarchy, the last card of German Imperialism in its attempts to forestall the revolutionary explosion of the proletarian movement.

The Hungarian Cabinet, at Tisza's demand, has been dismissed, and his servile follower, Baron Burian, has been appointed Minister for Foreign Affairs. Tisza is thus once again dictator — now no more under the Austrian Charles IV., but under the German William II.

Meanwhile, in Galicia, proletarian and peasant revolts are breaking out. The social traitors in Hungary are losing, with the fall of the Wekerle Cabinet, their last opportunity of carrying on the former policy of compromise. The feeling amongst the Hungarian workers is tense to the last degree, and the party leaders will not be able to avert a general strike. The Magyar troops, formerly, thanks to the assiduous agitation of the Nationalists, the worst oppressors of the Czech proletariat, have already become "unreliable." The Magyar detachments have now been replaced on guard by Tyrolese sharpshooters, not only at Prague, but also at Budapest and Vienna.

Count Tisza is officially the strategist of the Austro-Hungarian counter-revolution: but he is really the chief factor of revolution.

Germany, beyond all possible doubt, has reason to be afraid — and she is afraid. They have already tried the old method — that of concealing the danger: "Vörwarts" has been suppressed for a day. Not because it has dared energetically to raise its voice against the German Imperialists — those street-corner banditti; oh, no, that could not possibly happen with the

Scheidemann Party. But, only because the social-traitorous paper dared to say, very cautiously, that in Austria-Hungary the position had become serious, it was closed by the German censorship.

The German Empire is having recourse to the old methods of Tsarism — lies, and the suppression of any hint of revolution. But this will be of as little avail to save the situation, as the dictatorship of Count Tisza will be to help the Austro-Hungarian Monarchy.

These circumstances, on the contrary, are the best possible pledge that the Russian proletarian Republic is not waiting in vain for the international revolution. . . . In Austria-Hungary the crisis has matured.

The Moment at Penza

Far from the London cemetery with its grave covered by a plain stone slab, there has been erected, in the depths of the first proletarian State, the first monument to the first thinker and champion of the proletariat — the first public monument to Marx.

"Let us turn to Russia. The Tsar was placed at the head of European reaction. To-day he is a prisoner of the revolution, and Russia is in the front rank of the revolutionary movement in Europe."

These words, taken from the introduction to the second Russian translation of the Communist Manifesto, published under the supervision of Marx and Engels, have now passed into reality. Though continuing but painfully in the great struggle, surrounded by a ring of the imperialist executioners of all countries, the proletarian Republic remains the living proof of the truth of the Marxian teaching.

All the distorters of Marxism, traitors to the work of the proletariat in Russia as in Western Europe, the social-traitors and Mensheviks of all shades, are following the progress of the revolution, and the work of the organs of proletarian dictatorship, gnashing their teeth. But the proletariat, erecting a monument to Karl Marx, has left behind these semi-revolutionaries; and now this first stone monument is a splendid and visible demonstration of the fruitful propagandist work of the Communist Party in Russia.

However high the cultural level of the German or French proletariat, the scientific theory of the class struggle has not entered so deep into their soul as it has in Russia.

Even if the mass of the Russian proletariat was as "dark" as the leaders (without followers) of social-democracy are screaming in impotent fury, yet, in the task of awakening class-consciousness in the working-class, the proletarian revolution has done more than the propaganda of all the opportunists — now the deadly enemies of the revolution — taken together. The class struggle has reached the highest degree of intensity in which it was conceived by Karl Marx. The proletariat has organised itself as the ruling class, in spite of all the attempts to hinder it on the part of the social-philosophers, semi-philosophers, and aesthetes.

For the proletariat as a ruling class, a monument to Karl Marx is a monument to its own final victory. Thanks to this victory, Marxism in Russia has ceased to be the affair of intellectual study-circles whose intention it was to alter that teaching as it seemed good to them. The Marxian theory has become the accepted doctrine of the proletarian State, which was born of the revolution, and which continues it. If only because the dictatorship of the proletariat is carrying through the revolution to its logical conclusion, Marxism in Russia will not become an "offficial" theory in the sense in which it became such amongst the German Social-Democrats. Marxism was and is the theory of the revolution, just as Marx himself was never *merely* a theorist, but a revolutionary champion of the proletariat who always stubbornly fought for its victory.

The revolutionary class can never fall into the error of worshipping of individuals. Nevertheless, what one of the greatest Marxian economists said is true: "Names are factors." The same can be said of monuments. If the victorious Russian proletariat erects monuments on all its squares to its greatest fighters, this will be not the cult of individuals, but an act of respect towards its own revolution. And even if the priceless treasures of art disappear into the melting pot, it will not be barbarism, as some gentle souls affirm. Everything must be subordinated to the end of the proletarian revolution, just as everything hitherto was subordinated to the purpose of enslaving the proletariat.

The first monument to Marx, unveiled at Penza, is

assisting the work of the revolution, since the memory of Marx, in common with all his writings and actions, is in all its forms a factor in the victory of the proletariat.

Two May Days

One is the First of May of the victorious proletariat, already organised as the ruling class. It is the holiday of the proletariat which is being attacked on all sides by world-capitalism, which sees in it the greater danger. . . . But this holiday already celebrates a victory over the Russian capitalist class, and heralds the final victory over the capitalists of the whole world. Of the propertied classes we make no demand but this: *to disappear, and as quickly as possible*; but we make this First of May demand of Imperialism the world over.

Such is the First of May in every corner of the Russian Federal Soviet Republic — the First of May of the proletariat which has attained dictatorship.

Miserable slaves, groaning under the scourge: wretched beings, threatened by the sword and the rod: proletarians living in constant deadly fear, seeing nothing before them but the Imperialist slaughter — such is the First of May of the proletariat of other countries. . . . They are celebrating the international holiday of proletarian solidarity in the trenches and dugouts, like primitive men, who lived in caverns.

This picture is supplemented by another, serving as a background for the first. The First of May of the workers, employed in different branches of war work, enslaved, living under the threat of the lash and the knife of the capitalist class.

With their own hands they are turning out the weapons of murder and destruction, the weapons of their own oppression. Crushed by military and police oppression, drunk with the intoxicating flattery of their own traitor-leaders, overwhelmed by want and remorse for their treachery, they begin to revolt: for they are the forerunners of revolution.

There are two May Days: one the holiday of the proletariat which has never abandoned its thoughts of the

25

revolution, the other the holiday of the workers who have renounced the revolutionary methods of the proletarian movement.

The seeds of these two kinds of May Day were sown as far back as 1889. At Paris there were sitting in reality two international congresses at the time when the First of May became an international holiday. One of these parallel congresses was even then composed of the opportunist working-class leaders, whose lower middle-class minds were never able to understand the revolution, who could never clearly picture to themselves the final liberation of the proletariat from the yoke of the capitalist class. The leaders of this congress were the French Possibilists and Hyndman, who, in the end, became the servant of English Imperialism. The other congress was sitting under the spiritual guidance of Frederick Engels, then still alive. This was a different kind of Labour Congress, which in effect began the international May Day holiday, as the first, if still a weak, attempt at proletarian mass action.

The two congresses united; and the spirit of Engels, uniting with that of the first congress, in consequence, underwent a process of gradual corruption.

Two May Days were created. On the one hand, meaningless demonstrations: on the other, demonstrations with a new meaning, calling for a revolutionary struggle against militarism in addition to the old struggle for an eight-hour working day.

The spiritual heirs of the international congress of Possibilists and Hyndmans intended not only to distort the meaning of May Day, but even to bring about its disappearance. The Legiens and Bernsteins of various countries — the Trade Union bureaucrats and the revisionists — sought to efface the very memory of revolutionary tendencies in the Labour movement. And when the trustified unions of Imperialist enterprises began to use the anti-militarist May Day demonstrations as a pretext for dismissing the demonstrating workers, the official "leaders" of the working-class began trying to adapt both themselves and the Labour movement to the Nationalist requirements of Imperialism — thereby condemning the First of May to extinction.

The two May Day holidays which are celebrated at the present time arose out of the two sides oaf the Labour movement described above. One has resulted in the solemn celebration of the victorious revolution by the Russian proletariat; the other has brought only the trenches, the holiday of a proletariat collapsing under the police lash.

To-day's May Day is throwing light upon the shattered Labour movement. The old International, the first act of which was the introduction of this international holiday, has fallen asunder. In all the countries of the Imperialist world there has appeared a differentiation between the revolutionary proletariat and the social-traitors. The powerful working-class organisations have split: on one side, the revolutionaries; on the other, the men who desire to remain slaves.

This cleft in the Labour movement is a pledge of the re-establishment of international unity. The falsifiers of Marxism, who have distorted the "Communist Manifesto" to allege that the history of social progress is the history of the class struggle except during periods of war, have not only become generals without an army, but have ceased to be leaders altogether. They are nothing but charlatans, supported by the capitalist class, and animated by the intention of blinding the workers. But the stupor of the working-class is coming to an end. The salvation of the Russian proletarian revolution will come under the blows of international Imperialism.

The International being born at to-day's First of May holiday will, in virtue of its very essence, be neither the instrument of capitalist peace nor the weapon of capitalist war — despite Kautsky's deception of himself and of the masses. This International will itself be a new war — an international civil war; it will be the further guide and support of the Russian

Socialist revolution.

We can understand impatience in expecting the international revolution. Revolutionary Russia has already done such a great deal towards the liberation of the workers of all countries, towards the international revolution, that the workers of the world will never be able to give it all the thanks that are due. But any admission of pessimism on the part of the proletariat of revolutionary Russia would be treachery after the manner of the western European Labour leaders.

May each of these First of May holidays serve as a living symbol! One of them — the holiday of the Russian workers — the victorious May Day — serves as a symbol or example of the beginning of the reign of Socialism.

The Western proletariat will not be able to evade its historical destiny: it must become revolutionary.

The May Day of 1918 will be the last of the series of dual First of May celebrations. It will be followed by the true May celebrations of the victorious, ruling proletarian class.

This May Day is not only a symbol, but a signal. It is the symbol of the existence of the International, the signal for the world-revolution.

Marx and the Middle Classes

"The internal enemy" of the proletarian Russian Revolution is constituted first and foremost by the lower middle classes. The expropriation of the expropriators being carried out at present does not represent the most serious obstacle in the path of proletarian dictatorship. In the path of the expropriation of capital the obstacles are of a purely objective nature. The small group of large capitalists has not the masses on its side, and therefore speedily becomes powerless in face of the armed proletariat. The lower middle classes of society, on the other hand, represent a considerable section of the population, especially in Russia — to say nothing of the propertied section of the peasantry. To reckon with the wishes of these lower middle classes would mean the halting half-way of the work of the Revolution: it would mean an end of the aspirations towards the destruction of capitalism.

Exactly because the lower middle-class mass is numerically large, it has retained an influence over the working-class movement. But every concession to this influence represents a departure from the Marxian standpoint, because it was precisely Marx who freed Socialism from lower middle-class adulterations.

The behaviour of the middle-class Socialist parties during the opening encounters and the final decisive struggle of the proletarian revolution doubly imposes on us the duty of recalling, on the occasion of the centenary of the birth of our first teacher, what his views were on the subject of the lower middle classes. And, though the representatives of various shades of lower middle-class Socialism are constantly referring to Marx, in reality there is no greater sacrilege than this.

I

After the revolution alike in Marx's philosophical world-concept and in his views on the material conditions of social production, he shook himself free of the last vestiges of Liberalism.

"The Poverty of Philosophy," from the economic aspect, and "The Communist Manifesto," from the political aspect herald the final liberation of Socialism from the last lower middle-class swaddling clothes.

The founders of scientific Socialism had not had as yet the experience of a revolution, but by the path of theoretical analysis they had even then succeeded in establishing the fact that, in the progress of the revolutionary movement, the dower middle-class can display itself only as a reactionary and Utopian factor.

This lower middle-class — as "The Communist Manifesto" proclaims — "stands half-way between the proletariat and the capitalist class. Being a necessary complement of capitalist society, this class is constantly being reborn." Composed of extremely mixed elements of the pre-capitalist epoch — the so-called "toiling intelligentsia," the lackeys of the capitalist class — this class was to be found, in France, in Switzerland, and to a certain extent in Germany, at the advanced posts of the revolution of 1848. According to "The Communist Manifesto," the Communists were to support the various party groupings of these elements, while the latter were in opposition, understanding clearly, however, that if the representatives of the lower middle-class were really revolutionary in sentiment, it was only when faced with their immediate descent into the ranks of the proletariat.

These hopes of the lower middle-class, little sanguine though they were, nevertheless were completely shattered. The revolution of 1848 clearly revealed the political bankruptcy of the revolutionary section of the bourgeoisie. That revolution laid bare not only their weakness, but also how dangerous they were to the work of the revolution. During the French revolution of that year, the proletariat was crushed, not by the capitalists, but by this very lower middle-class. "The small shopkeeper," wrote Marx in "The Class Struggle in France," "rose up and moved against the barricades, in order to restore the movement from the street into his shop. And when the barricades had been destroyed, when the workmen had been defeated, when the shopkeepers, drunk with victory, turned back to their shops, they found their entry barred by the saviours of property, the official agents of financial capital, who met them with stern demands: 'The bills have become overdue! Pay up, gentlemen! Pay for your premises, pay four your goods.' The poor little shop was ruined, the poor shopkeeper was undone!"

The lower middle-class is not fit to wield power, and a long government by it is unthinkable. This, first and foremost, for economic reasons: the small shopkeeper is the debtor of the great capitalist, and must remain in dependence on him as long as there exists the system of credit — which cannot be destroyed while the domination of private property continues.

The Imperialist era of capitalist production has fully justified this view of Marx's. If the democratisation of capital by means of joint stock companies — the wild dream of the distorters of Marxism — were an economic possibility, even then the majority of the lower middle-class shareholders would be powerless to govern society.

The roots of the dilemma created by Imperialism are to be found in the economic relations on which Imperialism is based. There are only two classes capable of governing: the class of great capitalists, and the proletariat.

Every compromise with the *upper* bourgeoisie is treachery to the proletarian revolution. Every compromise with the lower middle-class after the victory of the revolution would mean the restoration of the supremacy of the upper bourgeoisie — the restoration of capitalist rule.

31

The experience of the revolution of 1848 completely confirmed Marx in his conviction that the revolution can blazon on its banner these watchwords only: the complete overthrow of all sections of the capitalist class, and the dictatorship of the proletariat.

II

Within the framework of capitalist society, the lower middle-class is immortal. Not only do small traders and small producers, worshippers of the principle of private property and credit, inevitably ensure the existence of parasites on the social organism, as being causes of the dissipation and waste of social labour; but also from out of their midst there appear the bearers of a special philosophy, directed for the purpose of restraining the proletarian revolution.

"The lower middle-class," in Marx's words, "has no special class interests. Its liberation does not entail a break with the system of private property. Being unfitted for an independent part in the class struggle, it considers every decisive class struggle a blow at the community. The conditions of his own personal freedom, which do not entail a departure from the system of private property, are, in the eyes of the member of the lower middle-class, those under which the whole of society can be saved."

And this is the very reason why the lower middle-class masses are the most dangerous enemies of the dictatorship of the proletariat. They represent a very strong section of society. Their special interests are absolutely incompatible with the economic disturbances which are the inevitable accompaniment of transitional periods.

The disturbance of credit cuts the ground from under their feet. They begin shouting for order, for the strengthening of credit, in such a way that every concession to them leads in effect to a complete restoration of the old order.

The bearers of middle-class philosophy, who took up their stand as critics of capitalism in the working-class movement at the time when that movement was still in the stage merely of a critical attitude towards capitalism, and who brought in with them a peculiarly lower middle-class outlook, feel disillusioned when the era of decisive battle arrives. Their supremacy in the realm of ideas can continue no longer; while it is beyond their powers to free themselves from the lower middle-class-world-concept.

This is what Marx says in his "Eighteenth Brumaire," in which he gives a masterly analysis of this lower middle-class outlook, on the subject of these "representatives" of the Labour movement — or, to speak more correctly, of these leeches which have attached themselves to it:

"By their upbringing and individual position, the former can be as far apart from the latter as heaven and earth. What makes them the spokesmen of the lower middle class is the fact that their thoughts do not leave the path in which the latter's whole life moves, and that therefore they come, by a theoretical road, to the same problems and solutions as the lower middle class reaches in actual life. Such, in general, is the relation between the political and literary representatives of a class and the class itself."

Marx was merciless in dealing with this kind of poisoners of proletarian class-consciousness. The whole Labour movement ought to be the same. With the weapons of ridicule and hatred he fought against the "heroes" of the French social democracy of the time — the political movement which represented an unlawful union between the lower middle class and the proletariat.

He wished to separate the Labour movement from all lower middle class elements, because the lower middle class attitude — attachment to the idea of private property, more or less open striving to uphold credit, terror of every fundamental social disturbance — is in practice the greatest internal enemy of the proletariat and the proletarian revolution.

III

A proletarian dictatorship that betrays a readiness to make concessions to the lower middle class is threatened with destruction.

A working class struggling against the bourgeoisie "from below" escapes this peril more easily than a victorious proletariat. A proletariat fighting "from above," possessing State power, and grappling with the problems of organisation of production, is in a much more difficult position than a proletariat which has not yet attained victory. The working class itself is not yet free from all lower middle class habits of mind, while the mass of middle class parasites which lived on the back of the old order is now, equally ready to live on the back of the proletarian State.

The crushing of counter-revolution in Russia shows that, here too, the time has come when, as Marx says in "The Civil War in France," all sections of the bourgeoisie except the great capitalists — "shopkeepers, tradesmen, merchants" recognise that the proletariat is the only class capable of initiative in the sphere of social reconstruction. This means, however, that the same section of the lower middle class which "offered up the workers as a sacrifice to their creditors" will once again attempt to come to an agreement with its creditors.

While the lower middle class exists, it is not capable of renouncing itself, even if it does submit to the proletariat. Though incapable of independent resistance, it will nevertheless try by roundabout ways to distort the meaning and the aims of the Revolution.

If it once manages, under whatsoever disguise, to reappear in the arena of the workers' struggle, it will use all its energies to the end that it may remain the proprietor of its little shop, and the client of capitalism. It demands first of all "the re-

34

establishment of credit" — but this cry is, for the lower middle class, only "a disguised form of the cry for the re-establishment of private property."

The Revolution, when celebrating the centenary of Marx's birth, will not forget the sentence he passed on the lower middle class.

The Desocialisation of Minds

At Kieff, the gallows is the weapon used against the minds of the *German* soldiers who have been converted to Socialism and revolutionised. At Reval, mutinous *German* sailors have been hung.

Immediately behind the front line time is more valuable: there is no time to build gallows there, but the bullet is quite sufficient. There it is bullets which are prescribed as remedies for revolutionary minds.

Nevertheless, the devastation in human material wrought by the war has been so great that the German and Austro-Hungarian imperialists, though they make use of gibbets and bullets, are forced to attempt to use the moral weapon also in the struggle with the minds converted to Socialism. In this way a new phrase has been coined, to describe the counter-revolutionary agitation in Germany and Austria-Hungary. This new phrase is "desocialisation of minds."

In Austria-Hungary the revolutionary "danger" is extremely strong. There the layer of workers bought over by means of the surplus value squeezed out of debtor States is considerably thinner than in Germany. It was there, therefore, that German militarism first gave the order to desocialise minds.

The pamphlets about the Bolshevik Government disseminated by the Ministry for War amongst the ranks of the Austro-Hungarian Army, represent an attempt to paralyse the influence of the Russian proletarian revolution. As for the prisoners of war, the government of the Dual Monarchy has had to give up all hope of them. The Government is so occupied by the struggle with internal collapse, it has become indebted to such an extent, that it has neither time nor money to spend on using these "spiritual" methods with the prisoners of war. Austria's only resource in this respect is the system of punishment camps which await all those returning from captivity; but hundreds of soldiers escape from these camps back to Russia, Ukraine, the Caucasus.

Germany, however, is a "cultured country" and a creditor State. Germany has both money and "spiritual" weapons for the struggle with the Bolshevik poison. She has not yet lost all hope of reforming her returning prodigals. The German prisoners of war are not less infected, but Germany is in a condition, at any rate, to create an apparatus for desocialising them.

The so-called "Chief German Commission," staying at present in Russia, has already been entrusted with the task of desocialising minds. It has brought with it informational material. The productions of German militarist literature will co-operate with the work of counter-revolution, with the object of restoring "voluntary" discipline, and, to quote from military regulations, the "self-reliance" of the troops if this is insufficient, gallows and bullets will be forthcoming, to desocialise for all time those minds which do not lend themselves to correction.

The diplomatic intervention of German imperialism hitherto relied on could, it is true, bring about alterations in the organisation of revolutionary agitation amongst the prisoners of war, but it was not in a position to prevent the revolutionising of minds. For this it would have been necessary not only to destroy the Revolution, but also to shoot the prisoners themselves.

The German imperialists cannot bring these methods to play; and for that reason — and for that only — they fall back upon the "culturo-informative" work of the German Commission.

Nevertheless, the "culturo-informative" work of the German counter-revolutionaries only assists the revolutionary work of the Communist emigrants from the Central Powers. This militarist propaganda attempts to restore "their native conditions" to the prisoners of war in Russia; and, according to advices from Minsk, Dvinsk, Vilna, and Przemysl, where concentration camps exist, escapes *en masse* are beginning. In this way the German and Austro-Hungarian proletarians will fly to Russia from under the yoke of German militarism.

German imperialism will be able to desocialise minds only by having recourse to the methods it has already tried in the Ukraine, at Reval, and at Vollmar: "Hands up!" and then the gallows or the bullet.

A School of Social Revolution

The counter-revolutionary forces have collected in force. It is quite comprehensible that, amongst the Russian proletarian masses, many should be awaiting the international revolution with impatience. Bolshevism is feeling the full pressure of persecution of the international counter-revolution because Bolshevism is the particular system of ideas which, represents the modern revolutionary movement. For the propertied classes, this system of ideas means deadly danger; for the Labour movement it is an inspiring and, creative force.

After the many buffetings of the war a considerable part of the Western European proletariat ended up in Russia. We may discover from the diplomatic notes of the German and Austrian Governments what these proletarians and workers have experienced and learnt.

We can see that the revolution has had an infectious influence upon these proletarians, from amongst whom large numbers have emigrated to Russia, when we consider certain phenomena, which might almost be called "mass phenomena."

Naturalisation into citizenship of the Russian proletarian State is a result of the influence of the revolution, although in some cases that naturalisation was prompted not by revolutionary motives, but by a kind of Nazarenism. A mere passively-resisting attitude towards the predatory aims of the imperialists — mere horror — does not represent the awakening of revolutionary consciousness.

But that is not the reason to which we can attribute facts like the events at Neriansk. There, during the course of several days, five hundred Magyar proletarians and workers became naturalised as Russian citizens, and united against the counter-revolutionary bands of Semenov. Amongst these revolutionary volunteers are many who, at home, never took part in the

Labour movement; and it is only the Russian revolution that has given them their Socialist education. Those who have participated in the propagandist work of the Social-Democratic parties cannot but agree that the educational significance of the revolution has attained unprecedented proportions.

Revolutions are the locomotives of history; not only in the objective sense, but also in the sense of their rapid development of the minds of the workers, within whom there takes place a process of deliberate re-examination of all previous values.

In this connection the letters received at the editorial and other offices of the foreign groups of the Russian Communist Party are not without interest. We shall quote a few passages from these letters to illustrate the educative influence, of the proletarian revolution. They were received by the newspaper "The Social Revolution," the organ of the Hungarian Communist group.

Here, for example, is the letter of a working man — of a miner. He is writing to his wife at Budapest, and sending a copy of his letter to the editorial office. In Hungary he belonged neither to the Labour Party nor to a trade union. He is now living at Kolchugina, in Siberia. He writes to his wife, *inter alia*:

"I received your past-card from Budapest, saying you had sent me 100 kronen. I haven't received them; but it doesn't matter, as I am working here and can earn enough to live on. But I am very sorry for you: how can you all manage to live on a quarter of a pound of bread? We, at any rate, are living in free Russia. What grieves me is not that I have to work in the depths of a pit, but that you are suffering. It's no good them writing in the papers that we've still got enough bread — we don't believe it! We know very well that not everyone is starving — Count Tisza and other gentlemen are not going hungry, of course, but the soldiers' wives and children are. Their fathers, after shedding their blood, have been left to suffer in Siberia, while the children, thanks to the lords and ladies, are starving. Oh yes, the workers can perish; so long as Count Karolyi, Lukacs, Kraus, and others can fill their pockets, it doesn't matter to them what happens to the wives and children of the men who were torn away from their families at the very beginning of the war to defend their "king and country." Now everybody's eyes are being opened, though. The capitalists can trumpet abroad as loudly as they like, that the Hungarian soldier was defending his fatherland: there aren't many who will believe it. Why don't they make peace? The Russian soldiers have all come back from the front. But the capitalists' pockets, I suppose, are not yet full enough, and so they've got to fight to the last Hungarian soldier. *I know it all, and so do others*!"

This is the letter of a "latter-day revolutionist."

Here is what workers write who at home took a more or less active part in the proletarian movement; two metal-workers from Budapest, at present employed at Linovka Station (Voronezh Province), who happened to receive one number of a newspaper published in Hungarian: "Your respected newspaper, after passing through hundreds of hands, has reached our remote little hamlet, where a few prisoners of war, amongst them Hungarians, are leading a monotonous existence. We read with great interest every line of the paper, and with every word there rose within us undying hatred and desire for vengeance — vengeance for those who have suffered agonies and poured out their blood on the fields of battle. . . . We longed for peace, and looked forward to returning. . . . But where shall we return? . . . You are quite right to say, honoured comrades, 'from captivity to prison.' But no, we cannot be blinded by 'defence of the fatherland.' . . . True, we weren't blind before, either: we were made to go. . . . "

The following passage from another letter shows how exactly that process begins, and the minds of working men, which leads to a clear and intelligent adoption of Bolshevik tactics, and how the idea of an armed rising, so foreign to all the western Social-Democratic parties, enters into the soul of the proletariat: "I assure you that I will only return to Hungary if the social revolution breaks out at home. In that case I shall hasten at once with arms in my hands to assist my struggling brothers against the imperialists. In my own country I belonged to the Woodworkers' Union, and here in Sarapul too." Here is the letter of a wheelwright and a mason, working at Akhtirka; in Hungary they were active party workers and agitators. They have become real and true Bolsheviks, as their letter shows: "We are very glad that you (Hungarians) have joined the Bolsheviks. Our return home depends on a revolution there. All we ask of our comrades is to write us immediately what form of activity we should engage in while we are staying here."

These extracts are in no way tendencious. They are snatches from letters taken from a very large correspondence. One may say that an overwhelming majority of the letters breathes forth not only a desire for peace on pacifist grounds, but also a will to, and expectation of, the proletarian revolution.

The mere appearance of this revolutionary will denotes a grave danger, not only for the capitalist class, but also for the opportunist Socialists. The revolution in Hungary will probably assume an anti-German character. German imperialism is the object of universal hatred amongst the Hungarian lower middle class, which, though not so numerous as in Russia, is still large enough to endow the revolution with a general nationalistic character.

But the school of the Russian revolution has created detachments which will be the grave-diggers of that nationalistic character, and may become the grave-diggers of capitalism. It would be difficult to imagine a school which taught better or more quickly. Those who hitherto had taken part in a Labour movement which was distorted by the lower middle class have now seen civil war at close quarters. Pacifism, which revolted against arms in general, and not against the arms only of the oppressors, has now lost its influence. In Russia the workers have learnt the usefulness of arms for attaining freedom, and the necessity of an armed rising for the purpose of conquering and swiftly shattering the power of the State.

The appearance of the grave-diggers of capitalism and social treachery will play its part; the Bolshevist advance guard is not only going to the help of the oncoming Hungarian revolution, but is itself preparing it for its work.

The Development of Revolutionary Forces in Austria

Everyone waiting impatiently for the international revolution should recall the events previous to the revolution of March, 1917.

In the attitude of the Austrian Government and the Emperor Karl we find an analogy with the state of affairs in Russia at that time. We must not seek such an extent of similarity as to amount to a complete coincidence of circumstances. We ought not to allow ourselves to be misled by the existence of the so-called Austro-Hungarian constitution. As is shown by the manifesto issued by the Austro-German Social-Democratic Party to protest against the postponement of the opening of the Reichsrath, Parliament has become a meaningless thing, inasmuch as the Imperial Government is quite incapable of sustaining Parliamentary criticism in connection with vital questions of Austrian policy, the organisation of the food question, the Imperial message, the resignation of Czernin, the broad questions of policy and finance of the Monarchy.

At the same time there is no bourgeois party which has not protested against the prorogation, of the Reichsrath. Various nationalist groups, amongst them a group of Czech deputies, have unanimously declared that absolutism is being set up, and have issued a protest against the Government. The fraction of German Social-Democrats has reminded the latter of Sturgck, laid low by the bullet of Friedrich Adler. *"If they take it into their heads, in order to please the Pan-Germanists who prolong the war, to re-establish absolutism and to govern Austria, by the methods of Störgck, then the working class will be obliged to rise and fight for the people's rights."* The manifesto calls upon all working men and women to remain in fighting order, so that at any moment they will be ready to join in the conflict.

On the other hand, facts are coming to light like the Report of the Commission controlling State debts, which actually deals with "sacred militarism" — the organs of the military system. Apparently the central Government was not able to prevent the appearance of this Report — in Austria, the classic home of the military censorship. Admitting that the issue of credit notes has reached incredible dimensions, the Report states that the feverish work of the bank of issue may awaken the most serious doubts from the financial, banking, and economic standpoint, and that the main reason for the particularly swollen demands of the War Department is constituted by "on the one hand, staff-officers' pay with war-time increases, which in the rear attains totally disproportionate rates; and, on the other hand, the uneconomical massing of troops behind the front. Finally, contractors are receiving excessive prices for supplies."

Who will not have recalled, reading this, the speeches in the Duma before the revolution, directed against the monarchical system? The bribery of officers by means of increased pay, as well as the massing of troops in the rear, are "inevitable and necessary" phenomena. The events at Trieste and Cracow show the necessity of collecting troops in the rear. The troops are so unreliable that the Government has to try several regiments before, at last, volunteers can be found to take upon themselves the repulsive "duty" of fratricide. At Trieste the town militia joined the participants in the hunger riots, while at Cracow the mob nearly managed to sack the military food dumps, until the authorities succeeded in bringing armed force to bear. There were even cases of street fighting. The risings take place without organisation, elementally; but from the point of view of the revolution, they have a symptomatic character.

Desertion is developing with gigantic strides in the Army; and it is measurable only by Russian post-revolutionary standards. From an order issued by the general officer commanding at Budapest, it is clear that soldiers in service battalions being sent up to the front desert in masses on the way.

The number of men arrested for desertion is so great that the military authorities have to make use of the civil gaols because there is no more room in the military prisons. This "uneconomical massing of troops in the rear" has become still more "uneconomical" as a result of the fact that, during the last brigands' attack on Russia, whole brigades and divisions had to be disarmed. When a small military detachment is required at least double the number of soldiers has to be sent: an unreliable regiment must be followed by a reliable one, which remains permanently in the rear: on the one hand, the lives of these reliable persons must be spared, while, on the other hand, all the reliability of these detachments would vanish into thin air if they were to be transferred from the rear to the front.

This is what is meant by the "uneconomical massing of troops in the rear," of which the Report of the Commission controlling State debts speaks. As for the food crisis, it is extremely characteristic that several districts in Austria have to be provisioned by Germany. Hungary is not providing bread for the simple reason that the ruling circles are not disposed to share it with others: the Hungarian well-to-do peasants have plenty of money. They hide their stores from the requisitioning commissions. The small peasant proprietors also defend their little surpluses from the gendarmes. Germany and Austria would only be able to receive food supplies from Hungary if they invaded her. Only by force could the Hungarian peasant be constrained to loyalty to his "Allies."

In Bohemia, as in Galicia, where hunger-riots have been suppressed only by main force, the ground is completely ready for a rising, in the districts populated not only by Czechs, but by Germans. An Extraordinary Congress of commandants of the German-Bohemian districts states in its resolution: "German Bohemia is at the last gasp."

The Tyrol lives only on German supplies, stolen in the Ukraine. Austria herself succeeds in stealing very little; and in this respect also Germany increases the degree of vassaldom of the Dual Monarchy.

The official Social-Democratic Party, which, it must be recognised, is at present beginning to drift to the Left, is still not the interpreter of the feeling of the Austrian working class.

From little notes which have escaped the Censor's eye we can ascertain that every market is a real battlefield — a battlefield in which men and women fight the police and the provisioning authorities. These conflicts are the accustomed daily event in every town. War industry is unstable, thanks to the "idleness" of the workers. Attempts are made — as, for example, on the State railways — to anticipate this form of silent sabotage where raw materials are concerned.

But nothing can be of any avail. In Trieste and in Cracow the workers have already taken up arms. *The weakness of the central government in Austria is merely a guarantee that the mass movement of the workers will one day pass, by means of an armed rising, into a victorious revolution.*

There is now no lack of activity.

The Model Product of Imperialism

A close alliance between Germany and Austria-Hungary has been concluded, and is making its appearance as a new factor in the arena of the world-war.

By this new treaty Austria-Hungary is annexed to Germany in the fullest sense of the word. If any of the nations that constitute the Dual Monarchy has recourse to a revolt or a rising, before it there will instantly rise the perspective of military occupation. The fundamental characteristic of the treaty, however, is not its reduction of Austria-Hungary to the position of a colony, not the economic exploitation of the country, but *the guaranteeing to Germany of cannon-fodder in order that she may realise her imperialists aims.*

Annexation is veiled in the form of a treaty: but this circumstance means nothing. The organs of the German military party do not attempt to conceal that that fact implies merely a special act of grace on the part of victorious German imperialism. The "Kreuz-Zeitung" points out that considerations of a military and political nature do not permit of the publication of the secret treaty, and announces triumphantly that the treaty of alliance between Germany and Austria is first and foremost the result of the German military successes. And the paper does not conceal the military and aggressive character of the new agreement; it does not hide the fact that its aim is the utilisation of Austro-Hungarian man-power for German military ends.

From the economic point of view, Austria-Hungary is completely exhausted. She can supply neither bread nor raw material. Its German imperialist allies have no longer any belief in its credit. The only article of commerce which Austria can still supply — albeit with difficulty — is cannon fodder.

Nevertheless, this treaty is meeting with no small

opposition from all the peoples of Austria, not excluding the German-Austrians. The "Arbeiter Zeitung" protests sharply against this aggressive alliance, this annexation; although the Austrian Government takes pains to emphasise that "the defensive nature of the Dual Alliance remains unchanged."

In spite of the desperate attempts to prevent the annexation and final reduction of Austria into the status of a colony, a semi-official statement of the Government has to declare, in discharge of "its duty as an ally," that the spearhead of this agreement is directed not only against Russia, as hitherto, but against "all other Powers." The semi-official statement of the Austrian Government goes on to point out that the new alliance, as it now stands, assumes the character of a "League of Nations" — under which title is masked a league of the Central European Powers, headed by Germany.

This may possibly pacify the Austrian social-patriots of the type of Karl Renner, but will in no way satisfy the proletarian masses of Austria and Hungary. Annexations will not calm the soldiers, deserting in larger and larger numbers, and, according to trustworthy information, refusing to go to the French front. . . .

If the Austrian semi-official statement twice emphasises the fact that "an unshakeable foundation has been created for the new alliance" — that military power which, in the eyes of the German papers, constitutes the chief value of the alliance — the Austrian monarch will not be able to do without the introduction of German troops into Bohemia and Hungary. Tisza and Seidler intend by means of this alliance to buttress the decaying fabric of the State; but the German imperialists will be able to force the Austro-Hungarian workers to observe the conditions of the treaty only by making use of the methods which were employed in the Ukraine.

The provisions contained in this treaty will be revealed only when the publication of the secret archives is accomplished in Austria-Hungary as in Soviet Russia.

The German, Austrian, and Hungarian revolutionaries must use the existence of the new alliance to increase their struggle against German-Austrian imperialism. The state of mind of the troops shows that that struggle has already begun. If there are still "Social Democrats" who, fearing an Austrian defeat, deliberately stand in the way of the revolution, they will be swept away by the masses of true proletarians.

After this treaty, the Austro-Hungarian proletariat is even more definitely than before at the cross roads of the dilemma: endless war or the revolution?

The Fruits of "Revolutionary" Chauvinism

I

"A thing, a phenomenon, may at one and the same time be both itself and something else." This dialectical axiom is justified by consideration of the Czech movement. That which in Austria is revolutionary, and which there is aiming at the overthrow of the existing order, in proletarian Russia is counter-revolutionary, in every sense of the word.

We are not speaking, of course, of Masaryk, that accomplished agent of Anglo-Franco-American imperialism, but of the Czech proletariat, at present passing through the stage of the national revolution — the stage in which, in the words of the "Communist Manifesto," the proletariat "fights not against its enemies, but against the enemies of its enemies . . ." Part of that proletariat, having found its way into Russia as a result of the imperialist war, becomes active in the capacity of a counter-revolutionary mass against the international revolution, and takes up arms against Soviet Russia.

This criminal activity of the Czech National Army cannot be justified by any revolutionary; but it is essential to understand it properly. It must be studied particularly in the interests of proletarian dictatorship — that beacon on which all revolutionaries fix their hopes. In spite of the personnel of the nationalist elements in the Bohemian revolutionary movement, in spite of the treachery of "Social Democrats" like Niemec and Soukup, in spite of all the circumstances indicated, this movement represents an active and important factor in the international revolution.

On the other hand, the events in Russia — the counterrevolutionary attitude of the Czech Army, 70 per cent of which are workmen — disclose a great peril. This peril threatens the social revolution not only in Russia, not only in Bohemia, but throughout Austria-Hungry. The counter-revolution which is threatening the railway from Penza to Vladivostok has its prototype in Bohemia and Moravia, in the persons of the nationalistic Czech bourgeoisie and the Socialist-tinted chauvinists of the type of Niemec, Soukup, and other leaders of Social-Democracy — none of them better than Scheidemann and Noske.

II

It should be observed that in the Czech Army, organised on the initiative of the National Rada of Masaryk and Co., all tendencies of the Czech Labour movement except the Centralists are represented.

The opportunism of the leaders of the Czech Social-Democracy, their complete estrangement from revolutionary Marxism, results, as far as the Austrian Government is concerned, in a tendency opposite to that which is noticeable amongst the overwhelming majority of the Austro-German Social-Democracy.

The Renners have become the greatest defenders of the Austrian imperial idea, while the Niemecs and the Soukups are its enemies. The result is the same, however: in both parties opportunism has led away from the international class struggle and towards a union of the social-patriots with "their" own bourgeoisie; a phenomenon which hitherto was peculiarly Austrian, but which during the war has become the general characteristic sign of all social-chauvinists; the phenomenon which Otto Bauer has named "pan-nationalism."

These Czech Social-Democratic leaders, who during the lifetime of Tsarism organised under Professor Masaryk's leadership a Czech National Army — making use of all the resources of terror and demagogy where the proletarian elements were concerned — had long ago lost all idea of the possibility of an independent movement of the Czech proletariat. Nationalism, revived by the opportunist policy of the "Social-Democratic" party and the trade union bureaucracy, swallowed up the remnants of the Socialist outlook on the world. There grew up a peculiar variety of nationalistic adventurism, similar to that which followed the revolution of 1848. (Karl Marx ridiculed and attacked it without mercy.) These hirelings of the capitalist class after the style of Kerensky sacrificed the Czech proletariat to Tsarism, and only the opposition of the overwhelmingly proletarian majority of the Army held them back, until quite recently, from coming out openly against the Russian proletarian revolution in the interests of international imperielism.

III

The more honest elements of the Czech proletariat have sunk as far as compromise with their own bourgeoisie and capitulation to imperialist agents only because they did not correctly gauge the strength of the Czech; capitalists. But class feeling must still be alive in these workers, because the different adventurers supported by imperialist gold could only carry on their activity in the name of Socialism. They made use of every form of Socialist artifice, beginning with "revolutionary-democratic labour organisations," and ending with the most Left, in order to betray the Czech workers to the nationalists. These hirelings of the oapitalist class have found an ultimate shelter for themselves in the bosom of the counter-revolution; but that criminal policy is cutting the ground from under their feet.

This disgraceful activity with which the masses of the Czech proletariat have spotted their good name, thanks to the demagogy of the nationalistic bourgeoisie, will be their last error. The suppression of this counter-revolutionary rising *will be brought about from within*; it will spring from the proletarian sections of the Army. These sections are now no longer swallowing the bait dangled before them by the capitalists, nor yet that offered them by their "Socialist" leaders. This counter-revolutionary movement will, in all probability, produce detachments to defend the independent action of the proletariat, not only in the Czech, but also in the general Austrian revolution.

That action is inevitable. Where Bohemia is concerned, we foresee quite clearly not only the development of existing forces, but also the course of the revolution itself. Police "pacifications" have done all that they can do; the masses have risen, and the Austrian Government will be hard pressed to find a reliable army capable of crushing the revolutionary movement. Courts-martial are of no avail. The power of the State will none the less continue to become weaker; and this circumstance will strengthen the revolutionary movement in other parts of Austria-Hungary.

The aims of the revolutionary masses in Bohemia are very confused; they leave much to be desired. The responsibility for this lies primarily upon the members of the majority section of the Czech Social-Democratic Party, who, like the Russian Mensheviks, have been quite unable to grasp that a bourgeois revolution is to-day quite unthinkable, as Marx expressed it in his "18th Brumaire." These social-traitors, like their supporters, the soldiers of the Czech Army in Russia, looked on the class struggle of the Russian workers with the capitalists as "fratricidal war of the Slavs," and wished to preserve their neutrality to such a degree that, by a logical process, they finally arrived at the stage of open counter-revolution. About a month ago the various Niemecs and Soukups amalgamated their party with the National Socialist Party, which had always fought under extreme jingo watchwords. In spite of this, they emphasised, in their colourless resolution, that "they stand for the principle of the class struggle" and that "between the Czech proletariat and the capitalists there exist class antagonisms." The whole course of the negotiations shows, however, that amongst these leader-traitors there is not one who thinks of an independent proletarian line of action in the oncoming Czech revolution.

The Czech bourgeoisie knows very well how to divert the proletariat from its own real aims, and how to use it in the interests of exploitation. Furthermore, Masaryk and his school have taken up their stand very close to the position of the semi-Marxian "lecture-room Socialists." The more danger that the absence of any independent line of action of the Czech Social-Democracy may be used to the end of awakening nationalistic hatred and crushing the Czech revolution.

If it is true (and it is unquestionably so) that the success of the revolution can at the present time be guaranteed only by independent action on the part of the proletariat, then that principle, as far as Austria is concerned, is doubly correct. Only such action can completely safeguard the solidarity of the workers of the different Austro-Hungarian nationalities; only such action is strong enough to neutralise the agitation, the jingo speeches, and the attempts at enslavement, of the German and Magyar capitalist class. It falls to the lot of the Czech proletariat to take its place side by side with the German and Hungarian workers, as the revolutionary advance-guard of Austria-Hungary; while the Czech Scheidemanns in Bohemia, as in Russia, are acting in direct opposition to this destiny.

The class-conscious elements of the Czech proletariat, like the other sections of the Austro-Hungarian labour movement, must have recourse to the most drastic measures to put an end to this disgraceful activity in Russia. The road to that end is disclosed by the "Communist Manifesto," and by the experience, based upon it, of the revolutionary Communist Party in Russia. Those groups and sections of the Communist Party which exist, legally or illegally, in Austria, must have the following character, in keeping with the words of the "Communist Manifesto":

"The Communists are, in practice, the most resolute and progressive section of the working class of all countries; from the theoretical standpoint, they have the advantage of understanding the conditions, course and general results of the proletarian revolution. The immediate aim of the Communists is the same as that of all other proletarian parties: organisation of the proletariat as a class, overthrow of the supremacy of the capitalist class, conquest of political power by the proletariat."

The Czech workers who, being in the ranks of their National Army, are thereby serving the interests of the S.R.-Cadet-Octobrist counter-revolution, are in reality the victims of the Czech "Social-Democrats" and emigrants in Russia — men who use the nationalist banner to prevent the organisation of the Czech proletariat as a class.

No mercy can be shown to these traitors, both there and here seeking to find a compromise with the bourgeoisie, and supporting the counter-revolution — at first under the cloak of neutrality, but now openly — just at the moment of the workers' greatest struggle. The Russian counter-revolution must be crushed as quickly as possible, in the interests of both the Czech and the world revolutions.

The Revolutionary Tide in Austria

The pulse of the Austrian revolution is daily beating quicker and quicker. The stormy tide of events is daily washing away more and more of the foundations of the existing order, constantly breaking off new buttresses. The governments rest within the country only on a thin crust. It has long lost all hope of the masses of the subject races: but it is now a question of lower middle-classes of the ruling races who are raising their voices against the new alliance with increasing energy. The Austro-Hungarian, and still more the Swiss, papers show us that, while the imperialist classes are closing their ranks around the German alliance, the mass of the lower middle-class is adopting a benevolent attitude towards the Entente Powers, trying to get rid of the war and of their ally, Germany.

The refusal of the war-weary soldiers on the Italian front to serve imperialist interests is a parallel phenomenon with that of the new orientation of bourgeois circles.

In Bohemia, and amongst the Jugo-Slav bourgeoisie, there has long been evident a current hostile to German imperialism. The same tendency is becoming more and more clearly marked in Hungary.

Count Karolyi, the leader of the most left bourgeois opposition and of the pacifists, has protested very sharply in the Hungarian Parliament against the alliance with Germany. In his speech he alluded to the whole dynasty in a tone unusual for Austria.

After this Parliamentary outburst, which found a wide echo in the country, Governmental circles have begun a campaign against him on the ground of alleged high treason. Proceedings have been begun in the Budapest Courts against Karolyi on the basis of a charge of having compromising relations with Italian statesmen. It is characteristic that materials for the case have been collected by the agents of the German General Staff.

The unreliability of the troops has increased by now to such an extent that, after Charles' visit to Constantinople, Turkish troops appeared in Austria-Hungary as the only trustworthy reserve against the internal as against the external foe.

Against the extremely unsuccessful attempt to introduce State Capitalism, after the manner of Germany, there is arising the opposition of not only the workers but also the lower middle-class, so numerous in Austria. Both in Austria and Hungary commercial conferences were recently held of the lower middle-class, whose existence is threatened by State capitalism. In spite of all attempts by official circles to moderate their fury, they more than once raised their voice against the Government, and protested against German colonisation of Austria.

On the other hand, the harvest has been requisitioned in advance, for the needs of the whole of Central Europe; a measure which has evoked from amongst the peasantry an unheard-of strength of resistance. This has determined largely the agitation amongst the troops on the Italian front, as they consist, for the most part, of peasant elements.

Side by side with this, the labour movement in Austria-Hungary is swinging more and more to the left. Even the party leaders, though badly infected with social-patriotism, have nevertheless become more radical than the German Social-Democracy. A regrouping is going on of the Left, the completely radical elements of the working-class movement, to a certain extent still acting as the opposition within the old parties. Both in Austria and in Hungary there are now in effect two party centres.

The illegal sections of the labour movement are fed by mass desertions of the workers at the front and in the rear.

Those organisations are still further and further developed by returning prisoners of war. In reply to a question about the Hungarian Bolsheviks, asked in the Upper House, the Premier Wekerle replied that the Government was quite powerless in this respect, as the elements infected with Bolshevism were returning home by routes of their own choosing, and avoiding the moral aid of the military authorities. Bolshevism is causing governmental circles, both in Austria and in Hungary, more and more anxiety.

The last hope of the reactionaries is that Count Tisza, who occupies a foremost position in the political arena, may, together with his agents Burian and Czernin, supplant the Premier Wekerle.

What the Austrian papers do not mention may be gathered from the small leaflets which are being circulated in Austria in the old, pre-revolutionary, Russian style. On their basis we can state that, within the frontiers of the Dual Monarchy, there are already dauntless champions of the international revolution. "The first problem is to save the Russian Revolution," says one of these illegal leaflets. "Its destruction would mean the victory of pan-European imperialism: its victory will signify the defeat of the latter."

These and many other symptoms show that there is already some sort of connection between the different outbursts of the revolutionary masses.

The lower middle-class mass is now not in the least intoxicated by military victories. The Turkish troops; the trials for high treason of leaders of the bourgeois opposition — all this shows us that military revolts and revolutionary strivings on the part of the workers and the oppressed peoples will not meet with hindrance amongst the lower middle-class mass".

Social-Traitors, Unite!

The Mensheviks, perhaps, may in the near future have the opportunity of realising the hopes ascribed to them in the bourgeois evening papers. According to the latter, these gentlemen intend to oppose the Bolshevik "terror" by an appeal to the public opinion of the International. An "International" corresponding to the Menshevik views is already in the process of formation.

Although the Dutch-Swedish commission, that abode of social-patriotism, has recently been dissolved — because, in the words of Huysmans, there is no hope of an International Socialist Conference in the immediate future — the fathers of social-treachery continue their activity. They are alive, and are again trying to organise a new "International," of the various social-Chauvinist parties, to "defend society" against the Revolution.

Kerensky's agent, Branting, will meet in London two "distinguished foreigners" — A. Thomas and Henderson, who did their utmost to hold in check the Russian Revolution. Vandervelde and Huysmans will take part in the conference. This "Entente International," whose greatest heroes — the late Ministers — will gather in London, will be a fitting body to respond to the appeal of the Mensheviks; for the former are just as much the enemies of the proletarian revolution as our own Social-Democratic pillars of capitalist society, recently excluded from the Soviets.

The Social-Democrats of the Central Powers, on the other hand, also lately carried on negotiations with the social-traitors of the Entente through the medium of Branting. The "tame" German Social-Democrats, together with the "official" Austrian and Hungarian Social-Democrats, received bulky packages from Branting containing materials for the forthcoming International Conference.

These preparations already give a taste of what wonderful perspectives will open before such a conference.

The Messrs. Legien and Co. have followed the example of the Russian Mensheviks. They have liquidated the German Social-Democratic industrial movement by amalgamating the "free" and "yellow" Trade Unions. It is just this that the Mensheviks are doing in connection with the Russian Revolution. To transform the Labour movement into a non-party, emasculated mass, devoid of all class-consciousness — that is the method common to the Legiens and the Menshevik "workers' plenipotentiaries."

There can be no doubt that these twins, sons of one mother — Opportunism — will be able to find a common tongue. Those who became a hindrance on the path of revolution and coloured the German Trade Union movement yellow, must proclaim their solidarity with the social-traitors who not only place obstacles in the way of the working-class movement but actually attack the proletariat when it has won power.

"For God's sake, don't touch Capitalism!" This haunting appeal of the social-traitors to the working masses, and the watchword of their Russian brothers: "Back to Capitalism," represent only two different stages of development in the process of betrayal of the workers' interests.

The International is arising — to defend capitalism and counterbalance the proletarian revolution. We can rest assured that this time the imperialist governments will not refuse to issue passports.

"Social-traitors of all countries, unite!"

The Birth-Pangs of the Revolution

The communiques from the internal front of the Austro-Hungarian monarchy daily give us further and further hope. The defeat on the Italian front is not the result of the strength of the Italian Army. On the contrary, it is brought about by the sharpening of the conflict on the internal front. The troops which have fought blindly and senselessly for years, in the cause of imperialism, are now deliberately surrendering. In Austria-Hungary there has at last arisen a yearning for the defeat of one's own imperialism. This denotes already a high level of development of the revolutionary consciousness.

Simultaneously with the news of defeats on the Italian front information has arrived, from the internal front, concerning bloody repression in Hungary. "The factories are idle," declares the Premier Wekerle; "just at the moment when their intensive activity is required."

This is a patent symptom that, by the undermining of war industry, the workers are instinctively striking for the defeat and dissolution of the military State institutions of their "own" imperialists, in order to clear the path in this way for the revolution. The refusal to accord the most elementary rights to the proletariat raises these waves still higher. The immediate political cause of the recent explosion was the project of electoral reform proposed by Tisza, which annuls all the solemn promises hitherto given. All the efforts of the official Hungarian Social-Democratic Party were directed only towards the achievement of electoral reform. They were attempting to divert the working-class movement into "legal" channels, and thereby were hindering the development of the revolution. But objective conditions broke up these artificial channels, and the workers have begun to use semi-legal methods of struggle. The last events show us that the Government has to suppress the workers' revolts "with blood and iron."

At Budapest, where the movement assumed an extremely threatening character, the Government invoked the assistance of the gendarmes, of whose good offices they had availed themselves hitherto only to maintain order in the villages. In them lie all the hopes of the Government at the present moment, as it is no use counting on the soldiers: they are the worst firebrands of the revolutionary movement.

But the weapon is two-edged, and the repressions of the gendarmes render existing antagonisms still more acute. During the last demonstrations at Budapest four workers were killed, while the wounded are reckoned by scores. This measure will still more rapidly force the workers to forsake the peaceful path of the struggle for the franchise. From day to day the conditions for an armed uprising of the masses become more and more mature.

At Pecs, one of the principal industrial and mining centres of Hungary, the soldiers of the 48th Reserve Infantry Regiment shot their colonel and several officers. On the other side of the Danube, in Western Hungary, the soldiers secretly removed from their barracks arms and ammunition.

Returned internationalist prisoners of war, carrying on revolutionary agitation, are subjected to the most savage persecution.

The Government may possibly improve the economic position of the workers to a certain extent; but politically it is quite incapable of making the slightest concession to them. The composition of the Governmental parties precludes the possibility of any modifications whatsoever in the Tisza-Wekerle project of electoral reform. In those parties are represented not only the semi-feudal aristocrats, but also the rich peasants and manufacturers, compulsorily organised nowadays into manufacturers' associations.

The new project for the compulsory amalgamation of large industrial enterprises, the indirect tax on corn, and the mill monopoly, as a means for uniting the financial and landed aristocracy — all this reduces the proletariat to a condition from which no electoral reform can rescue it. Thanks to this condition, all sections of the lower middle class, as well as the proletariat, have been brought to a state of desperation.

The country has been handed over, lock, stock, and barrel, to the German militarists. The promises and pacifist declarations of Count Czernin could only for a short time keep the people in a state of deception, even with the efforts to the same end of the official representatives of the working-class movement.

The recent meetings and strikes, however, prove that the masses are about to take over the question of peace into their own hands.

That is a sketch of the general situation in Hungary. The new Minister of the Interior is trying to calm the frightened bourgeoisie by telling them that the soldiers' mutinies will be suppressed by the most drastic means. But there are no longer any reliable troops available for this purpose. In one small town in Bohemia, lately, the following incident occurred. The 68th Infantry Regiment, which hitherto had been considered trustworthy, and which was specially ear-marked for the work of crushing the Czech revolutionary movement at Prague, suddenly went over to the side of the workmen on strike.

The new alliance with Germany is reviving the movement in the Austrian half of the Dual Monarchy as well. The unsuccessful offensive against Italy is there, too, bearing its revolutionary fruit.

The condition of the Austro-Hungarian monarchy clearly points to the fact that the birth-pangs of the revolution have begun.

The Revolution in Hungary

The working-class movement in Austria-Hungary previous to the risings already bore all the signs of developing revolution. The Austro-Hungarian and German papers give us only fragmentary information about the revolutionary movement which has sprung up. But even from that we can make two important deductions concerning the strength, the power of resistance, and the meaning of the revolutionary movement.

First, the strike in Hungary is not a purely local event. It is not a series of strikes embracing separate industries. It is *one mass movement, bearing the stamp of the General Strike*, in the sense that *work has ceased everywhere, in all the most important branches of industry, transpot, and mining*.

Secondly, it is absolutely impossible to reduce the causes for the General Strike purely to hunger or the demand for electoral reform. *The General Strike is directed against the machinery of the State* — against militarism and discipline.

All the demands of the strikers are connected with the question of power, and, as such, rise beyond the limits of the parliamentary State. The movement, it cannot be doubted, will not continue on the scale of the usual mass strike, especially as it is fraught with the most deadly peril for the vital interests of a State at war.

The movement has adopted the typical forms of that stage of a revolution which is the forerunner of the actual rising. Here and there more and more frequent cases of stoppage of work are to be observed, representing something unheard of during the first three years of the war — right up to the October Revolution. The "union sacrée" has been smashed to atoms by the workers themselves. All attempts at conciliation on the part of the leaders of the official Social-Democracy, whose aspirations have never left the bounds set by a narrow Parliamentarism, have beeen in vain.

True enough, the proletarian movement arose elementally; the strikers have not a clear class feeling or a concrete social policy; the movement has no leaders, and is semi-conspirative; but it is undoubtedly revolutionary. Greater results have been achieved than by the last forty years' struggle for the franchise.

In their search for the path to freedom, the workers have entered the trade unions. Before the war, the membership of the Hungarian trade unions never exceeded 110,000; during the last two years, they have had an increase of over 100,000 members. During the war it was impossible to transform the labour organisations in accordance with the revolutionary requirements of the proletariat; but the *workers now are carrying on the struggle in spite of the trade union leaders*. The mass struggle has in Hungary become the accepted method of the working-class movement, even though it has not yet received official sanction. For fifteen long years the official organs of the Party have threatened the bourgeoisie: "We shall begin to talk Russian." At the present moment, the Hungarian proletariat is talking and, actually, acting Russian.

In Budapest there is a general strike. The railwaymen have struck. Other enterprises are on the eve. The postal and telegraph employees are adopting passive resistance, which is nothing but a veiled form of strike.

The chief coal pits are also idle. According to the declaration of the Hungarian Minister for Commerce, 600 truckloads of coal per dray are wanting through the strike at Petroszeny alone. The transport crisis has reached its maximum.

The workers openly refuse to obey the orders of the administrative officials of the militarised enterprises. They threaten the commandants and officers with the fate of the colonel at Pecs, whom the soldiers killed with their rifle-butts.

The repressive measures undertaken in the case of one individual workman, who had been arrested for a statement of this kind, served as the immediate cause of a strike in the largest mining district in Hungary. In Budapest, after an exchange of shots in the State railway shops, the workers sacked the office of another factory.

In the demands of the metal-workers' deputies, put forward on June 19th, the following two points appear: (1) The withdrawal of gendarmes from the factories; (2) The dismissal of the railway shop officials.

On June 21st the strike at Budapest *became a general stoppage*. The newspapers did not appear; the tramway services stopped; the postal and railway servants announced their solidarity with the strikes (a strong movement is noticeable in their midst); the private postal-telegraph-telephone services also ceased. The leaders of the Party and of the trade unions made an attempt to moderate the movement; but from day to day new proclamations appear, *calling on the workers to continue the strike*.

The Minister for Commerce and Industry has declared in Parliament that the action of the railwaymen and postal servants will be crushed by the most severe repressive measures. The Government wants to crush the working-class movement by violence. The proletariat must reply not by isolated shots, as happened lately at Budapest, but by a mass movement. The bourgeoisie can no longer rely on its military forces. The soldiers are going over to the side of the people, not only at Pecs, but also in other towns. In the Hungarian plain regular pitched battles between deserters and the gendarmerie have taken place. On the Italian front, the Hungarian troops — like the Roumanian, the Serbian, and the Slovak soldiers — either refuse to take the offensive, or else surrender.

The quantity of "trustworthy" troops is quite insignificant. On the other hand, the number of deserters and men arrested for violation of discipline is growing. *The*

Hungarian military prisons have long been so full that the authorities have been forced to make use of civil gaols.

Tisza has appeared in the foreground. Wekerle, the Hungarian Trepov, is still Premier, but Count Tisza has announced that the day is at hand when he will take over the government in order that repressive measures shall be ruthlessly administered. But whether Tisza will have time to do this is another question. The objective situation, in Hungary is such that there is little hope of governing by means of a Parliamentary ministry, and without an open dictatorship.

And from the open dictatorship of the capitalist class, it is not a long step to the open dictatorship of the proletariat.

The Foster Child of Monarchy

During the great French Revolution, the guardian of the principle of legitimity, of the principle of monarchy, was the Holy Roman Empire, as it was then — the Austrian Empire, as it is now. At the present time that part is being played by Germany.

All the present German Chancellors, whatever their name, strive to act up to the réle of Metternich, the Austrian Chancellor of that time.

But there is a fundamental difference between Germany now and the Holy Roman Empire then. The German Empire does not intend to reinstate the old dynasties; it founds new dynasties, setting on the throne its own representatives. The first such attempt has taken place in the Ukraine. In the person of Skoropadsky there is, in effect, at the the head of the State a Viceroy, with all the characteristics not of a constitutional but of an autocratic monarch. The question is whether Germany intends to set on the Ukrainian throne one of the "unemployed" still remaining Romanovs, or a German prince. The Romanovs would possibly find some adherents in the ranks of the Black Hundred; but the revolutionary movement in the Ukraine displays the necessity for a "completely reliable" German monarch, who would not under any circumstances show hesitation in crushing opposition.

We have seen the same picture in Finland. The former Grand Duke Cyril Vladimirovitch, a scion of the Romanov house, was amongst the spectators when, in the Parliamentary arena, the Duke of Mecklenburg-Schwerin was proclaimed King. In Finland, just as in the Ukraine, the restoration of the monarchy represents not merely the rehabilitation of the general principle of Monarchism, but the restoration of the bourgeois State as a whole, in contradistinction to the proletarian State.

In such a case the restoration means the withdrawal of power from a class which can take part in the work of government *only when it is in a position to become the sole master of that power, i.e., when it holds the dictatorship*. A return from the dictatorship of the proletariat to the monarchy can only be a symptom of a form of reaction which, in the end, will, notwithstanding, shorten the path to Socialism.

In future, Skoropadsky and the Duke of Mecklenburg-Schwerin can no longer be displaced by the Rodziankos, the Kerenskys, the Martovs: they can be displaced — and soon will — only by the dictatorship of the proletariat.

Materials for the History of the Birth of the Hungarian Revolution

The eyes of all workers are turned towards Russia. Mass emigations of the persecuted reach the Ukraine, but very rarely does anyone manage to reach Russia.

Lately a Hungarian metalworker visited our group. He had deserted from the Italian front, lived in an illegal position near Budapest, and then fled, on June 1st, through Bukovina and the Ukraine, to Russia. His comrade had served in a prisoners-of-war camp, and had picked up a little Russian from the Russian prisoners. They succeeded in reaching the frontier by means of false documents, which are easily procurable in Hungary. One of them has communicated the following to the newspaper, "The Social Revolution" — the Magyar organ of the Russian Communist Party — concerning the reasons which prompted him to start for Russia —

"I am asked why I left Hungary for Russia. I had my good reasons.

"Instead of the régime of Tisza, who was told to go to the devil in 1917, there appeared the far-famed 'democratic' government of Count Esterhazy. He displayed his zeal for democracy 'in practice.' He began negotiations with the leaders of the social-patriotic party, and begged them on his knees to support him in his work and make the working class realise that 'the fatherland' was in danger.' 'We are surrounded by enemies,' he told them. But he forgot to mention that the danger only threatened his family estates.

"He only underlined the necessity for increasing production, the reward for which would be universal and secret suffrage, including women in its scope. He promised to bring the Reform Bill into Parliament as soon as possible, in order together with it to confirm the war loans which were crushing the workers. 'We shall also assign you seats on the Food Commission at present being organised. After all, such a position is no mean one at a moment when there is no bread, and when we have to cudgel our brains to discover how to satisfy the demands of the mob for bread.' The Party leaders replied something after this style: 'Leave all that to us: we know what to do. Guarantee us a demonstration, which will give us a chance to throw light upon the political situation, and it will not be unsuccessful — Goodbye, Excellency.' The demonstration took place, but the expected 'success' was not forthcoming. Moreover, something took place which the worthy leaders had not even in their dreams expected.

"All the shop windows at the corner of Rakoczy Street and at the Royal Museum were smashed, so it appeared: the shops had been looted, and the goods taken home. This was rather too much . . . "Nepszava" shortly published an explanation, alleging that hirelings of Tisza were responsible for the looting: not sober-minded people, but ruffians hired by Tisza, to oust Esterhazy from the ministerial armchair. And that wasp not to be recommended: after all, it was only Esterhazy who could get the Reform Bill through . . . The arrests showed that the riot was not organised by hooligans bought by Tisza. It turned out that the arrested men were organised workers, who would never sell themselves to Tisza — as the leaders of the official party who had not gone over to Esterhazy pointed out.

"The distrust of the people towards the Party leaders from that day began to grow, and found expression in the January strike. The leaders had to resign, because the workers had become more class-conscious, and a crowd of 200,000 people was pouring through Budapest, intoxicated with the Russian revolution, and crying "We too want a revolutioin!" But the party leaders, who were negotiating with Wekerle, were not capable of that . . . Instead, they tried to bring confusion into the ranks of the proletariat. They allowed the tram-men to come out, but exacted certain sureties from the delegates of some of the workshops, and ultimately we had nothing left us but to stand by our sureties. Then they sent 24 of us from the workshop to the Italian front, whence I fled, via Budapest, Bukovina, and the Ukraine, to Russia.

"I will remark that we did not know that in Russia had been set up the dictatorship of the proletariat. Had that been known to us, our mass strike would have ended quite differently. They deliberately concealed it from us.

"During the January strike we had the opportunity of observing that the elements advocating revolution were for the most part young workmen, between 18 and 24. They defended the extremist point of view, declaring that what we needed was a revolution, not franchise reform. In March and April they were taken for the Army. The same fate threatened me, and I don't in the least regret having escaped it. I now have the chance of making a closer aquaintance with proletarian dictatorship; at home, in our wealthy capitalist country, it is only the labour leaders who cannot even comprehend it.

"I am happy to be able both to observe and to fight for that proletarian dictatorship, and, spiritually enriched, to return home to open the eyes of the workers, starving in our rich Hungarian land of Canaan, concerning the enormous difference between a demonstration in the name of electoral reform, and the dictatorship of the proletariat.

"Will anyone, after all this, ask me why I fled from Hungary to Russia?

"With fraternal greetings, Tanczicz."

In this letter is reflected the state of mind of the Hungarian proletarians, previous to the great June strike.

Marxism Versus Social Democracy

Address delivered at Plenum Executive Committee of the Young Communist International

Comrades,

March 14th, 1933, marks the fiftieth anniversary of the day on which humanity lost the most important mind it has ever possessed. Karl Marx, originator of Communism, founder and leader of the International Workingmen's Association, the man who gave the proletariat "the consciousness of its own position and needs, the consciousness of the conditions of emancipation," died on March 14th, 1883. In the workshop of this mind was created *the most potent, most complete and most comprehensive* work to be found in the history of humanity.

Marx's doctrine is the most potent doctrine because it is the reflection of the objective truth. It did not proceed from any theoretical principle with its nucleus born in the "realm of reason" in order to draw its further conclusions from this principle. On the contrary, by their content Marx's teachings are the theoretical expression of the real struggle which was going on in his day and is going on now in capitalist society with its anarchic mode of production, that struggle between those who possess and those who do not possess, between the capitalists and the wage-workers. They constitute the answer to questions raised by the foremost minds of humanity before Marx, but hitherto left unanswered. They are the answer to all the questions put by *an actual historical movement*, questions which we are being made hourly to face by the working-class movement of to-day.

Marx's doctrine is *the most complete* there is. It contains *the definitively discovered law of development governing human history*; which, as Frederick Engels said in his funeral oration at the bier of his dead companion in their joint labours and struggle, "contains the simple fact covered up under ideological over-growth that man must, before all else, eat, drink, live and clothe himself, and then only can he engage in politics, science, art, religion, etc.; that therefore the production of the immediate material means of existence and thereby the corresponding degree of economic development of a people or a period forms the basis on which the State institutions, legal views, art and even the religious ideas of the people concerned developed and on which they therefore must be explained — and not vice versa, as heretofore."

Marx's doctrine does more than expound the general law of development of human history. It also contains the *special* law of development of the capitalist method of production and of bourgeois society engendered by it.

The great secret of capitalist production and its concurrent bourgeois society was a sealed book to the best representatives of bourgeois economy who investigated the capitalist method of production and deemed it an eternal institution, as well as to be the best representatives of pre-Marxian utopian socialism who critisised and rejected the capitalist system. *The discovery of surplus value* by Marx revealed this secret of capitalist production and bourgeois society. The wage-worker in capitalist society sells his labour power to the owner of the means of production. It is not a question here of any *relation of things*: product of labour and means of production, but of *relations between people* of whom one has only his labour power while the other owns the means of production. Commodity labour power is endowed with the peculiar property that even when purchased at its full value it creates more value than the equivalent of its own value, *i.e.*, than is necessary for the reproduction of the commodity labour power. The private appropriation of these unpaid surplus values is the basis of the capitalist method of production and it is precisely this surplus value which is the source from which the capitalist class draws its growing wealth.

The discovery of surplus value led not only to the discovery of the motive power of the development of capitalist production, but also to the discovery of the driving force of the struggle between the two classes arising historically under capitalism: the proletariat and the bourgeoisie. Socialism was no longer a fortuitous discovery of this or that "gifted mind" but recognised as a necessary consequence of capitalist development and of the class struggle.

Capital — created by the workers — brings about the ruin of the small producers. It multiplies the class of the wage-workers. By developing the forces of production (machines, etc.), it constantly increases the earnings of the capitalists derived from the work of the former. Capital becomes more and more concentrated and finally leads to monopolist domination by a handful of the most powerful magnates. Production becomes more and more socialised. Hundreds of thousands and millions of workers are embraced in a few industrial organisations. The product of their social labour is, however, appropriated by a mere handful of capitalists.

In the process of the concentration of capital, human labour power is increasingly displaced by machinery. This leads, on the one hand, to the most intensified accumulation of wealth for the capitalists; on the other, to increasing misery for the working class. This also gives rise to the giant army of the unemployed. This *industrial reserve army* renders possible a still more intensive exploitation of the working class by the capitalists.

This constant expansion of production (which is accompanied by a steady decline in the purchasing power of the masses), leads to crises of over-production which become more aggravated at each repetition and shake the capitalist system more and more.

This historical tendency of development of capitalism was *strikingly* epitomized in "Capital," the main work of Marx, in the following words:

"The expropriation of the immediate producers was accomplished with merciless Vandalism, and under the stimulus of passions the most infamous, the most sordid, the pettiest, the most meanly odious. Self-earned private property, that is based, so to say, on the fusing together of the isolated, independent labouring-individual with the conditions of his labour, is supplanted by capitalistic private property, which rests on exploitation of the nominally free labour of others, *i.e.*, on wages-labour."

"That which is now to be expropriated is no longer the labourer working for himself, but the capitalist exploiting many labourers. This expropriation is accomplished by the action of the immanent laws of capitalistic production itself, by the centralisation of capital. One capitalist always kills many. Hand in hand with this centralisation, or this expropriation of many capitalists by few, develop, on an overextending scale, the co-operative form of the labour-process, the conscious technical application of science, the methodical cultivation of the soil, the transformation of the instruments of labour into instruments of labour only usable in common, the economising of all means of production by their use as the means of production of combined, socialised labour, the entanglement of all peoples in the net of the world-market, and this, the international character of the capitalistic regime. Along with the constantly diminishing number of the magnates of capital grows the mass of misery, oppression, slavery, degradation, exploitation; but with this too grows the revolt of the working-class, a class always increasing in numbers, and disciplined, united, organised by the very mechanism of the process of capitalist production itself. The monopoly of capital becomes a fetter upon the mode of production, which has sprung up and flourished along with, and under it. Centralisation of the means of production and socialisation of labour at last reach a point where they become incompatible with their capitalist integument. This integument is burst asunder. The knell of capitalist private property sounds. The expropriators are expropriated."

Even thirty vicars ago these words read like a prophesy, but to-day they already *toll the death knell of moribund capitalist society and sound the tocsin of the attacking proletarian armies* which, in the midst of the devastating world economic crisis, are storming the fortresses of capitalist exploitation and oppression on the sure ground of the post-war crisis of decaying capitalism. These prophetic words, the recognition, too, of the laws revealed by them, have brought it about that *socialism which was a utopia has become a science and finally a reality*, a science which records the objective law of development of society to socialism as dictated by nature.

Therefore the doctrine of Marx is the most complete which has been created through the collective efforts of the thought of all preceding generations and through the genius of their individual thinkers.

Marx accomplished the discovery of the general laws of motion of the development of human history as well as of nature through the cognition of *materialist philosophy*, on the basis of the cognition that, as Feuerbach said, "thinking is to be explained from being and not being from thinking." Marx, however, did not stop at this general cognition. Dialectics — the science of the laws of the development of the external world as well as of human thinking which was liberated by Marx and Engels from the idealist envelope of the Hegelian system of philosophy — in its materialist form — the doctrine of the relativity of thinking as a reflection of matter eternally in motion — confronted Marx with the question whether different stages in the development of society had not different and peculiar laws of motion. Marx discovered the peculiar laws of motion the capitalist method of production and of bourgeois society built upon it.

Yet he went farther than that. In contradistinction to everything that had existed before him in science, Marx's doctrine is not only an *explanation* of society, of its objective laws of motion, but is simultaneously the doctrine of the transformation of society.

In the notes by Marx on Feuerbach penned in the Spring of 1845 when, together with Engels, he wrote "German Ideology," which was both the foundation of Marxism and the balance sheet, if you like, presented to bourgeois ideology; we read:

"The philosophers only give different interpretations of the world, but the point is to *transform* it."

The doctrine of Marx is the first not only to give a world outlook which is not only a *Weltanschauung*, a world philosophy, but a doctrine of the *transformation* of the world and *a guide for effecting this transformation.*

It consists not only in that which the materialists taught even before Marx, namely that

"Man is a product of circumstances and upbringing; modified man is therefore a product of other circumstances and changed upbringing."

"Circumstances are modified by man," reads the great, historic, epoch-making discovery of Marx, by which not only was philosophy freed from the shackles of intuitive materialism but theory also — through materialist dialectics — was transferred to *practical, human, perceptible activity.*

"Man himself makes his own history" is what the great discovery of Marx denotes. The recognition of this fact has made *active agents* out of the proletarians instead of merely *passive* ones.

Society divided into classes accomplishes its development in the class struggle. The class struggle is the basis of its development. The class struggle is the driving force in the history of humanity.

The proletarians have not only been changed from passive to active agents but from *active individuals to exponents of their class and its consciousness.* Thus Marx developed the kernel of his doctrine.

MARX'S TEACHING ON THE WORLD HISTORICAL ROLE OF THE PROLETARIAT AS CREATOR OF THE NEW SOCIETY

In his letter to Weydemeyer, dated March 5th, 1872, a year after the Paris Commune, the first revolution of the proletariat, Marx himself described this kernel of his doctrine in the following manner:

"What I did was to prove, first: that the existence of classes is linked only to definite historical stages of development; second: that the class struggle leads necessarily to the dictatorship of the proletariat; third: that this dictatorship itself forms only a transition to the abolition of all classes and to classless society."

The historical rôle of the proletariat, as the creator of the new society, consists therefore in the conquest of its own class dictatorship, as the pre-condition of the abolition of all classes and the creation of classless society.

Thus the most important point was discovered: the path to Socialism, the path to the liberation of the proletariat, the direction of the leap humanity must take from the land of necessity into the realm of liberty, into socialism.

The science of Marxism is likewise "an historically moving, a revolutionary force." Science and revolution are united in Marxism not through the personal qualities of the creator of the doctrine, but internally and inseparably through the method — through *materialist dialectics*. Therefore Marxism is not only the most potent, the most complete, but also *the most comprehensive* of all doctrines that have been created in the field of the cognition of nature and of human society.

This most potent, most complete and most

87

comprehensive of all doctrines, which itself represents an historically moving, revolutionary force, is *the theory of a class*. It lays no claim to hovering above the classes. It lays no claim to being non-partisan science, without pre-conditions. It is the theory of the revolutionary class of the proletariat and its *revolutionary class party* — the Communist Party!

Let toothless Kautsky repeat a hundred and a thousand times that the doctrine of the dictatorship of the proletariat is not the quintessence of Marxism; let his disciples keep on repeating after him such chatter as that the dictatorship of the proletariat was a "youthful aberration" of Marx and Engels. Marx himself attests the fact that his doctrine can only be the theory of the revolutionary workers, of the party that struggles for the dictatorship of the proletariat and materialises it.

The revolutionisation of the working class, the historical mission of which is the revolutionary overthrow of existing society, could only be effected by anchoring socialist theory in the consiousness of this very class. On the other hand, the transformation of utopian socialist theory from an "absolute truth," "independent of time and space and historical development" and which only needs be discovered in order to "conquer the world by its own power," into a *science*, could take place only by connecting socialist theory, on the very real basis of the existing capitalist system, with a definite class in whose very interests it is to fight for the destruction of the capitalist system and for socialism, *viz*., the working class.

The socialist movement and the labour movement pursued parallel and separate courses before Marx. The more or less sectarian socialist trends and movements lived their own lives outside of the working class and its daily struggles. The labour movements, the struggle of the workers against the employers, even the struggles of the workers for political rights (as for instance the Chartist movement in England), proceeded without being given socialist aims. Socialism and the working class, the socialist and the labour movement, were united for the first time by the party whose theoretical and practical leaders were Marx and Engels: by the revolutionary party of the Communists. This party was first the Communist League, whose programme was the Communist Manifesto dawn up by Marx and Engels.

The other revolutionary labour organisation called into life directly by Marx and Engels was the International Workingmen's Association, the First International, the first world party of the revolutionary proletariat. The following historical slogan in its constitution has since become the common property of the international working class:

"The emancipation of the working class must be accomplished by the working class itself."

But the interlinking of socialist theory with the labour movement could not be consummated through revolutionary theory alone. That required also a revolutionary leader.

"Marx was a revolutionist above everything else," wrote Engels. "To participate somehow or other in the overthrow of capitalist society and of the state institutions created by it, to participate in the liberation of the modern proletariat . . . was his real life profession. And he fought with a passion, ability and success that could be matched by few."

As a revolutionist Marx was the "most hated and most slandered man of his day." And this not only as the mortal foe of the bourgeoisie who called and organised the workers for combat. He was hated and spurned as an enemy not only because he was the leader of the Communist League, the editor of the revolutionary *Neue Rhenische Zeitung*, the founder of the First International, the leader of its General Council, the advisor of the socialist organisations and movements in Europe and America, the leading *publicist* of the revolutionary labour movement, the spokesman of all revolutions of his day before the forum of international public opinion: of the French, the German, the Austrian and Hungarian revolutions in 1848-49, of the French Commune in 1871, of the revolutionary movements of the Russian Naródniki in the '70's and 80's, the defender of the oppressed nations: the Poles and the Irish as well as the Hindus and the American Negroes, but also because he fought against petty-bourgeois democrats like Mazzini, Ledru Rollin, Kinkel, etc., who in the name of the "interests of democracy" attempted to prevent the development of an independent Class Movement of the Proletariat. He was no less hated and slandered as a fighter against the world-redeeming ideas of the various socialist and anarchist sects, from Weitling and Proudhon by way of Willich, Schapper and Bakunin right to Ferdinand Lassalle, the friend of Bismarck. They all wanted to transform the world either according to their own ready-made prescriptions or to tie the working class to the tail of the ruling classes.

"The history of the International," wrote Marx, on November 13th, 1871, to Boltke "was a continuous struggle of the General Council against the sects and amateur attempts, which sought to assert themselves against the real movement of the working class within the International itself."

The *Right-opportunist, petty-bourgeois danger* (to use present-day terminology) which greatly threatened the young class-conscious labour movement from its inception, encountered his passionate ire in no lesser degree. In his famous *Critique of the Gotha Programme* he warned the follower of the Eisenach tendency of the dangers of the Lassallean dilution of the German labour movement. Together with Engels he remonstrated still more energetically when during the period of the validity of the anti-Socialist law the delivering over of the Party organ of the German Social Democratic Party to a circle of friends consisting of "philanthropically-minded students and professors of the upper and lower middle-classes," was contemplated.

"So the gentlemen have been forewarned," wrote Marx in 1879 to Sorge on the occasion of the emergence of this

90

opportunist danger, and they know us sufficiently well to appreciate that here it means either *bend or break*! If they want to compromise themselves, *tant pis* (so much the worse).

"In no event will they be permitted to compromise us."

An irreconcilable revolutionist, hurling defiance at all governments, whether absolute or republican; at all bourgeois-conservatives as well as extreme democrats, all petty-bourgeois — the preachers of general fraternisation between man and man, as well as the preachers of general destruction — inflexible revolutionist was our greatest of teachers, Karl Marx.

The fifty years that have elapsed since the death of Marx have been a period of incessant struggle *for and against Marxism*. No matter how numerous or how palpable the evidence furnished by history to corroborate the correctness of Marxism, the struggle for and against Marxism has never stopped, as this struggle is part of the great contest between two historical classes, the class struggle between bourgeoisie and proletariat.

As these fifty years rolled by, the course of historical development not only fully and completely confirmed, in the countries of older-established capitalism, the soundness of the Marxian teaching, but it was confirmed also by *the awakening of new classes* in the East — in Japan, in India and China — which had been only partly covered by Marx's investigations and whose "historical inactivity and sleep" were of great assistance to the bourgeoisie of the old capitalist countries in maintaining their positions against the working class in their own countries.

The historical tendency of capitalism's development, that is the ultimate passing beyond that stage of society, has moved towards its end with the iron necessity predicted of it by Marx and Engels. Capitalism, which after Marx's death had already subjugated the entire world, entered *a new phase* at the end of the nineteenth century, the phase of *monopoly capitalism*, of *imperialism*. Through the concentration of capital in the hands of a few cartels, trusts and syndicates, dominated by still fewer major banks; through the seizure of the sources of raw materials especially in the colonies; through *finance capital* whose international cartels have commenced the economic partition of the world among themselves, free competition was replaced by monopoly. The export of capital became the principal means of the expansion of capital. The territorial division of the world among the great imperialist powers was concluded. In one imperialist war after the other (the Spanish-American war of 1899, the Boer war of 1900-02, the Russo-Japanese war of 1904-05) history was confronted with the problem of a fresh *division of the world*.

The three peculiar features of imperialism — *monopolist, parasitic and decaying capitalism* — have evoked a number of far-reaching changes in bourgeois society. The bourgeoisie of the imperialist countries has lost the last remnants of its progressive rôle. All its sections — though they harbour antagonisms among themselves — have become *reactionary*. The parasitism of the bourgeoisie, enhanced through the formation of an entire section of *rentiers*, has not only strengthened *political reaction* but also corruption, which had already assumed tremendous proportions. The parasitism of the ruling class has reached a monstrous scale through the export of capital and the exploitation of the *colonies*. The bloodsucking bourgeoisie in every imperialist country has extended privileges to an upper layer of the working class, the *labour aristocracy*, which occupies its privileged position partly at the expense of the colonial peoples, partly at the expense of the native proletariat. In the Federal Council of the English Section of the First International "a vote of censure was administered to Marx because he said that the English trade union leaders were bribed." But this reprimand has been rescinded by history. The *labour aristocracy*, a bribed section of the working class, has become an international phenomenon. To the extent that the English working class *as a whole* lost its

92

privileged position through the shattering of England's Monopolist position on the world market, the bribed section of the *labour aristocracy* took shape in the other imperialist countries as well.

The *decay of capitalism* through the monopoly system — as well as the sharpening contradiction between the growing socialisation of labour and the capitalist method of appropriation — meant that capitalism, as Marx had predicted, was entering the stage of its death throes.

The monopoly system within the framework of an unevenly developed world capitalism placed two decisive questions upon the agenda of history: imperialist war for a division of the world and proletarian revolution for the dictatorship of the proletariat as the transition, to socialism!

Marxism and the class movement of the proletariat, on reaching this turning point in history, have arrived at what is a critical stage for themselves. The laws of motion underlying capitalist production discovered by Marx, and of bourgeois society corresponding to this *mode of production*, have exerted their influence on a higher plane of development. The historical fate of capitalism having entered a decisive stage, the historical destinies of Marxism have also entered a sphere marked by the embittered struggles of historical decisions.

Marx's doctrine went through its historical development in the smoke of battle, both while Marx was still alive and after his death. Before the bourgeoisie applied the *criticism of the weapon* as such, or force of arms, against the revolutionary labour movement, it endeavoured to destroy Marxism through the *weapon of criticism*. An entire caste of doctors of philosophy, university lecturers, professors and syndics representing capitalist interests and independent scholars, an entire caste of large and small-scale producers of bourgeois ideology, was formed to "kill off" Marxism. They not only "killed off" Marxism daily, weekly and monthly in their periodical and non-periodical publications, but they buried it just as often. These "Marx-killers," these economic and political weather-prophets of the bourgeoisie, applied their learning mainly against the law of the concentration of capital, the law of the pauperisation of the working class. Every reform, however small, every achievement of social policy, however petty, which was gained by the working class in severe class struggles was celebrated as a refutation of Marxist teaching, particularly that concerning the class struggle.

The influence of bourgeois ideologies upon the working class was not only fostered from without, but also *from within*. In the *pre*-imperialist period of capitalism this influence was exerted mainly through the medium of the proletarianised artisans, through *newcomers* in the working class. During the period of imperialism the *labour aristoracy* became the principal intermediary through whom bourgeois influences penetrated the working class.

Marxism after the dissolution of the First and the formation of the Second International gained the *hegemony* in the struggle of the working class to bar bourgeois influences from its movement. In the comparatively "peaceful" period after the overthrow of the Paris Commune until the Russian Revolution of 1905 and the beginning of the evolutionary movements of the Eastern nations, Marxism expanded the positions it had won among the broad masses. The perfectly obvious facts of the real development of the class struggle under capitalism were far more potent than the "proofs" of the Marx-killers.

Other methods had to be applied against Marxism which was deservedly extending and strengthening its hold among the working class.

Along with the method of *Marx-killing*, the method of *Marx-adulteration* had to be resorted to, mainly within the labour movement. By this means it was hoped to create a bourgeois labour movement instead of the proletarian-revolutionary class movement of the workers.

94

"The dialectic of history is such," wrote Lenin in his article entitled *The Historical Fate of Marxism*, "that the theoretical victory of Marxism forces its enemies to don Marxian garb. Internally decaying liberalism seeks a revival in the form of *socialist opportunism*."

After the death of Engels the Second International entered upon this stage of Marx-adulteration on a "wholesale" scale, entered upon an "entire stage of the undivided domination of opportunism." Upon the structure housing the leading party of the Second International, the German Social-Democratic Party, the lately deceased Edward Bernstein openly hoisted the flag of the revision of the Marxian doctrine. In the realm of *philosophy*: against materialism, for idealism; against the "traps of Hegelian dialectics" — "back to Kant." In the realm of *economy*: against the Marxian theory of value, for its "supplementation" by the so-called theory of final utility of Boehm-Bawerk's Austrian school of economy, a theory which attempted to refute the theory of labour value. In opposition to the doctrine of the concentration of capital, a theory concerning the "indestructibility of small-scale production" and the "democratisation of capital" through joint-stock companies, was created. A theory concerning the absolute and relative amelioration in the position of the working class was counterposed to the theory concerning the absolute pauperisation of the working class. Whole libraries were written by Edward David and other revisionists "to prove" that Marx's teaching had no application to the development of agriculture. In agriculture small-scale production gains the upper hand over large-scale production — was the conception of the revisionists.

The Marxist *theory of crises* was singled out for special attack by all the revisionists who maintained that capitalism through its cartels, trusts, etc., had overcome its anarchy and thereby also its periodically recurrent crises. By overcoming these crises and thus preventing the return of catastrophic mass unemployment, by dint of the increasing "social consideration of the bourgeois class," which finds its expression in the

95

strengthening of social policy — through all, this Marx's "theory of collapse" was to be disproved. It was claimed that revolution would no longer be necessary to overthrow the rule of the bourgeoisie; that no dictatorship of the proletariat was necessary to safeguard the transition from capitalism to socialism; that peaceful reformist work, the conquest of a parliamentary majority on the part of the Social-Democratic Parties, would assure *evolution into socialism*. Socialism was to cease to be the cause of *one class*, of the working class, and was to become the product of the peaceful "collaboration of all classes of the population." In this way socialism was to be withdrawn as an urgent actuality of the hour which had to be faced just when it had been raised as a living issue by the advent of imperialism. "The final goal means nothing to me — the movement is everything," was the motto of Edward Bernstein, the revisionist.

But the most dangerous falsification of Marx was not open revisionism, but the "defence" of Marxism by the Marxian Centre under the leadership of that driest of pedants, Karl Kautsky, Pope of the Second International. This "defence" consisted in the abandonment of what were just the most important theoretical positions of Marxism in favour of the revisionists this being done primarily on the issue which the revisionists put metaphysically as: "*Reform or revolution.*"

Marxism was to be split into two parts: into its "revolutionary" and its "reformist" ingredients. Reform as such held an *independent significance* all its own in the theory of the Centrists. Reforms were divested of their real character of a by-product of the revolutionary struggle and set up as a goal in themselves. The first victim of the "defence of Marxism" by the Centrists was the *Marxian theory of the State*. The doctrine of the dictatorship of the proletariat, and, therefore, Marx's doctrine of revolutionary tactics, as well, was relegated by the Centrists to the attic of history as something superannuated. What Marx and Engels had written about armed uprising was passed over in silence or destroyed as so much "Blanquist deviation." Engel's introduction to Marx's *Class Struggles in France* was brazenly falsified by the representative of the Executive Committee of the German Social-Democratic Party by suppressing those passages that spoke of armed uprising. Centrism was far from being headed towards a struggle against the bourgeois influence that the revisionists allowed to seep in; it represented, on the contrary, *conciliation* with the transformation of social democracy into a bourgeois labour party.

Revisionism and Centrism are most closely interwoven on the question of imperialism. For both, imperialism was not a *special phase* of capitalist development but *a policy* of part of the ruling class. The one openly espoused the imperialist policy of its own bourgeoisie, the other did the same thing while making a pretence of combating imperialist policy by mouthing pacifist phrases.

The left radical tendency, headed by Rosa Luxembourg, conducted a valiant struggle against revisionism and centrism, but not consistently against the latter. She was not in accord with the conciliatory attitude of Kautsky and Bebel toward Bernstein and Vollmar. The left radicals demanded the expulsion of Bernstein from the Social-Democratic Party. But they themselves designated very important theoretical views of Marx as "erroneous" or "obsolete." They did this in the case of the law of the accumulation of capital; in the case of the doctrine of Marx and Engels concerning the national question and the peasant question; of their (Marx's and Engels') views concerning the rôle of the proletarian party, concerning armed uprising, the dictatorship of the proletariat, etc. It therefore could not be the tendency which continues Marxism in accordance with the new phase of the capitalist development of imperialism. It therefore was incapable also of discovering the *roots of revisionism*. For it *reformism* — and that variety of revisionism known as centrism — was not an inevitable consequence of the social composition, the social stratification, of the working class, but in large measure nothing but a theoretical or political deviation of individual theoreticians or leaders of the social-democratic parties.

This was the situation in the Western Sections of the Second International when imperialist development confronted the proletariat with two vital questions: *imperialist war and proletarian revolution-imperialism or socialism?*

The passing over of the revisionists as well as the centrists to the side of their own bourgeoisie, their attitude in favour of the imperialist war (in form openly social-chauvinist or mantled by social-pacifism), and their abominable betrayal of the cause of the working class was *conditioned by the entire preceding development of the Second International.*

The Left radicals, in accordance with their previous principles, conducted the struggle against imperialist war with courage and self-sacrifice. Liebknecht, Luxemburg and Mehring will live for ever in the history of the labour movement as courageous and valiant revolutionary fighters for the cause of the proletariat. Yet, and this was in keeping with their attitude on very important theoretical questions of Marxism, they could not break with the centrists during the war and even after the war they could do so only after a struggle, for they were not consistent supporters and continuers of the work of Marx and Engels. When the laws of motion of capitalist production and bourgeois society, laws discovered by Marx, were being "refuted" in whole or in part by the dominant tendencies in the Western parties of the Second International, it was naturally impossible to perceive that capitalism had entered a new stage in conformity, with these laws. Nor could they perceive what constituted the peculiar traits of capitalism during this phase and what conclusions the proletarian parties had to draw therefrom. The perception of the imperialist phase of capitalism and of its special traits reached on the basis of Marxian dialectics and the special laws of capitalist production discovered by Marx — this historical, epoch-making perception could rise only in the mind of a Marxist who permitted neither so-called "criticism," nor "supplementation of Marxism," nor its ossification into a lifeless dogma.

THAT MARXIST WAS LENIN!

Only Lenin could succeed in accomplishing this epoch-making discovery: only he was the one consistent continuer of the Marxian doctrine after the death of Engels. He alone could show the right path, tell the working class how it should act in this new imperialist phase of capitalism, especially with reference to imperialist war.

He perceived reformism in its every variety, whether revisionist or centrist, as an inevitable phenomenon of capitalist society and completely exposed its social roots: the petty bourgeois sections of the proletariat which had sunk down to the working class and the sections of the proletariat that had risen to the labour aristocracy — there was its social source.

He also perceived the historical significance of reformism from its inception in whatever variety it appeared, revisionist or centrist. In 1908, in his article dedicated to the twenty-fifth anniversary of the death of Karl Marx, he gave final shape to the characterisation of reformism as follows

" . . . . It is quite natural that the petty bourgeois world outlook should again and again break into the ranks of the broad workers' parties. It is quite natural that this should be so, and it will always be so, until the climax of the proletarian revolution; for it would be a great mistake to think that the "complete" proletarianisation of the majority of the population is necessary in order to bring about such a revolution. What we now experience more often on the mental plane only — discussions with theoretical additions to Marx what now emerges in working practice only on certain particular questions of the labour movement as tactical differences with the revisionists and splits on these grounds — the working class will have to experience to an immeasurably greater extent when the proletarian revolution makes all debatable questions acute, concentrates all the differences upon points which have most direct significance in determining the attitude of the masses and compels us, in the heat of the battle, to separate enemies from friends, and to expel bad allies in order to deliver decisive blows against the enemy."

Leninism, which according to Stalin's classic definition is "Marxism of the epoch of imperialism and of the proletarian revolution" was born in the struggle — *in the only consistent struggle* — for Marxism against the "Marx-killers" as well as against the Marx-falsifiers, the "supplementers" and "critics" of Marxism. Even *historical continuity* exists between the activity of Frederick Engels, Marx's peer as a collaborator and comrade-in-arms, and *Lenin*, their peer as a continuer of their work and struggle.

Frederick Engel's activity was terminated in 1895 by his death. In 1894, *Who Are the Friends of the People and How do They Struggle against Social Democracy?*, the product of young Vladimir *Ulyanov*, appeared illegally in Tsarist Russia in hectograph form. In this early work of Lenin's, Marxism appears *in full armour*, the programme of the Communist revolution stands forth in complete and bold relief in a "way" that no one except Marx and Engels had ever presented it. In this work he took up the cudgels, not only against the special Russian form of petty bourgeois socialism, against the Nardóniks, but also "against the narrow conception of Marxism . . . . even among the Marxists." Two years after the death of Engels appeared the protest by Lenin and his colleagues against Bernstein and his Russian supporters, a protest written while in Siberian exile. This protest, in contradistinction to the "defence" of Marxism by Kautsky and Co., really and consistently defended Marxism in its entirety and in *every particle of its doctrine*. From this first hectographed production of Lenin's until the October Revolution and until his last work, which dealt with the co-operative plan, the same consistency in the development of his original thoughts may be noticed as with Marx and Engels, and their first labours until the last words written by them.

The October Revolution, the dictatorship of the proletariat in the Soviet Union, the construction of socialism throughout one-sixth of the globe, commenced under the leadership of Lenin and continued under the leadership of Stalin, is the fulfilment, the materialisation of Marxism in a struggle, not only against the bourgeoisie, but also against the opportunism of the Marx-falsifiers — which had developed into social-chauvinism, social-imperialism and social-fascism, from Bernstein, Kautsky and Trotsky to Otto Bauer, Hilferding and Vandervelde, as well as against the Right and "Left" distorters of Leninism.

The greatest historical act accomplished after the October Revolution in the course of socialist construction, the rooting of socialist forms in agriculture resultant on the achievements of socialist industrialisation (effected through the collectivisation of the peasant farms and elaborated theoretically and practically by Stalin), is nothing more nor less than a literal materialisation of that which Marx and Engels thought and wrote concerning the transition to Communist economy. In a letter, heretofore unpublished, written by Engels to Bebel on January 20th, 1886, we read the following concerning Marx and Engels' plan of collectivisation

"And that during the transition to Communist economy we will have to utilise collective economy as a medial stage on an extensive scale, neither Marx nor I ever doubted. Now matters must be so arranged that society, i.e., in the first place, the State, retains the ownership of the means of production, (Compare The Nationalisation of the Land, the latest decree of the Soviet Government concerning the inalienability of collective-farm land and concerning the machine and tractor stations — B. K.), and that the special interests of the collective as against society as a whole cannot become incrustated." (Compare, again, the purging of the collective farms of the kulak elements that had crept in, as the result of the efforts to sabotage grain-collections. — B. K.).

If we juxtapose the documents saved from the literary heritage of Marx and Engels and published recently — documents which were kept secret by the excellent premonition of social-democratic theoreticians like Bernstein and Kautsky — to the works of Lenin and Stalin, the fact must be acknowledged that the theoretical and practical attitude of Lenin and Stalin on questions in which the opinion of Marx and Engels could not have been known to them completely coincides with the attitude of Marx and Engels, in many instances even *verbatim*. This is not merely a matter of the personal qualities of Lenin and Stalin which can be measured with the rod of our two old masters, but the proof that the Bolshevism of Lenin and Stalin represent the only consistent continuation of the work of Marx and Engels.

Developments during the fifty years that have elapsed since Karl Marx died have not only fully and completely confirmed, upon a new stage of their development, the laws of the capitalist method of production, discovered by Marx, but especially their theory concerning the State and revolution, the dictatorship of the proletariat, as the only possible way to socialism. Not only the tremendous development of the forces of production through the dictatorship of the proletariat in the Soviet Union, but also — and this is especially to be noted at the threshold of the second Five-Year Plan — the struggle to train the toilers to become conscious builders of classless society confirm completely what Marx and Engels set forth in their "German Ideology," published recently for the first time:

"That for the mass generation of this Communist consciousness, as well as for the accomplishment of the matter itself, a mass change in man himself is necessary, which can only take place in a practical movement, in a revolution; that the revolution, therefore, is not only necessary because the ruling class cannot be overthrown in any other way, but because only in a revolution can the overthrowing class reach the point of ridding itself of all the old rubbish and of becoming capable of founding a new society."

In the struggle between the two systems — capitalism and socialism — the banners of the proletariat, which has become the ruling class, bear the proud slogan of the Communist Manifesto:

Workers of the World, Unite!

The leader of the proletarians of all countries, the Communist International, has it in its charter that:

"The Third Communist International, founded March, 1919, in Moscow, capital of the Russian Socialist Federative Soviet Republic, declares solemnly to the entire world that it undertakes to continue and conclude the great task begun by the First International Workingmen's Association. "

This pledge to complete the work of the First International of Marx and Engels is an undertaking to fulfil, to materialise Marxism, begun by the October Revolution under the leadership of Lenin, a materialisation to be accomplished by incessant, arduous and indefatigable struggle for the world dictatorship of the proletariat. Marx belongs to those who fulfil his teaching, who struggle for the materialisation of Marxism — to the Leninists.

Marx belongs to us!

To us, the Communist International and the Young Communist International!

III.

Many of you will consider we are being too fervent in stressing so sharply the fact that Marx belongs to us.

Who besides Communists lays claim to Marx to-day?

Was it not Mr. Emile Vandervelde, chairman of the

Second International and repeatedly Minister of His Majesty the King of Belgium, who recently publicly repudiated Marxism?

He did this by replying to a new "Marx-killing" by *Lord Melchett*, chairman of the English Chemical Trust, better known as Sir Alfred *Mond*, partner to the English reformist trade-union leaders in founding so-called *Mondism*, the English variety of the theory of industrial peace. This noble lord said about seven years ago and reprinted in his book, entitled *Industry and Politics*:

"If there is one thing in the world which is dead in this country it is socialism. It was buried at Liverpool, buried deep, deep down. You have only to read Mr. Ramsay MacDonald's speech to all. And why? Because every practical man knows, and every man who has had the responsibility of Government in this country, knows perfectly well in his heart, whatever he may in theory think about socialism or speak about it, you cannot apply the system. "

To this Marx-killing the chairman of the Second International replied as follows:

"Socialism and Marxism are not to be taken as synonymous. . . . It would give the conception of socialism a peculiarly narrow construction if this conception were to be completely identified with Marxism. "

The chairman of the Second International had nothing else to do but feign that he was abandoning the "sinking ship" of Marxism, his life he had boarded perhaps once only as a stowaway.

Was it not Karl Renner, one of the most prominent theoreticians of Austrio-Marxism and former Chancellor, who, on the hundredth anniversary of the birth of Ferdinand Lassalle — whose doctrine concerning the State became the socialtraitors' theoretical point of departure — stored away Marxism for good when he wrote:

"Marx was right when figuring in centuries, but when

figuring in the decades in which we live, Lassalle was right in every particular. "

Both statements appeared in the theoretical magazine of the German Social-Democracy, edited by Dr. Rudolf Hilferding.

Another star of Belgian Social-Democracy, Henrik de Man, highly esteemed as a theoretician in the entire Second International, declared in his book *On the Psychology of Socialism* that "the vanquishing of Marxism, " "the liberation from Marxism" were the result of his work. To him this vanquishing of Marxism is "not only a question of knowledge, but also of conscience" (German: "Wissen" and "Gewissen"). He does not any longer want to support. the lie — he writes this himself — that he is a Marxist as his party comrades do; he does not want to participate in the hypocrisy that is being practised in Germany where, in his judgment:

"Properly speaking Marxism no longer has any internal points of contact whatever . . . with the trade union and the co-operative movement, at least not in the sense that it directs their activity . . . . It only continues to play a rôle in the political activity of the Social-Democratic Party, which is recognised by the party as useful (*i.e.*, for the purpose of "Left" manœuvres. — B.K.). Social-Democracy is constrained to conduct an opportunist policy of coalition and support of the State, which, while not in reason, yet in sentiment contradicts the prior keynote of irreconcilable class struggle to which it owes its origin; in consequence of which it is particularly interested in emphasising the inner stability of this policy by symbolising its attachment to the Marxian tradition . . . It (*i.e.*, Marxism. — B. K.) can no longer guide the policy of the party because this policy rests upon actual pre-conditions, which contradict those out of which the doctrine once arose. Of course, Marxism can still supply slogans for agitational purposes, slogans which, in the main, bridge the gap between the political tradition of yesterday and the policy of to-day. "

This is the judgment of a leading social-democrat, not

only concerning Marxism in general but also concerning the *relation between social-democracy and Marxism.*

In his latest book on *Capitalism and Socialism After the World War* (Rationalisation — Mistaken Rationalisation) (Fehlrationalisierung), Otto Bauer "dethrones" the Marxian theory of price to replace it by a brand new "theory" of Marshall, Moor and other American investigators of busiess conditions and manufacturers of ideology for Dollar Imperialism:

"The significance of these investigations is just as great for the development of the theory of price, " wrote Otto Bauer, commenting on the work of these American economists.

"Heretofore the function of demand was no more than a mathematical symbol of the given demand situation which the price theory utilised to represent schematically the dependence of the market price upon the given demand situation. Only when definite functions for individual commodities, calculated on the basis of statistical data, take the place of the symbolic functions do we attain an inductive-statistical price theory."

The price theory of Marxism, based upon the doctrine of value promulgated by Marx and Engels, is therefore declared *inadequate* by Otto Bauer and is "supplemented" by a vulgareconomic theory. Naturally, the only effect achieved thereby is a new "refutation" of one of the most fundamental precepts of Marxism.

And was it not Mr. Tarnow, a prominent leader of the A.D.G.B. (General German Trade-Union Federation) and of the German Social-Democratic Party who eliminated Marx altogether in his book *Why be Poor?* He actually accomplished the feat of raising Henry Ford, the auto king, to the rank of theoretician of the reformist trade-union movement, in order to prove that socialism was unnecessary, as poverty could be abolished forever under capitalism by using Ford's method.

Tarnow wrote

"Henry Ford's book, *My Life and Work*, is certainly the most revolutionary writing of all economic literature to date."

Thus in the reformist trade-union movement Marx's *Capital* — written *against* capital — had to yield place in revolutionary world literature to make room for Henry Ford's book — written *for* capital.

While Otto Bauer repudiates Marx's theory of price, Rudolf Hilferding, who before the war was engaged in revising Marx's money theory, cannot now reconcile himself to Marxism as applied to the agrarian question. On the occasion of the agrarian debate in the German Social-Democratic Party (1927) he declared in his *Theoretical Observations on the Agrarian Question* that:

". . . the dispute concerning the preponderance between large and small-scale production in agriculture continues *undecided* to this day . . ." That on the one hand; and on the other he says that: "precisely the application of Marx's method" shows "that the law of concentration (*i.e.*, the law concerning the concentration of capital and of enterprises) does not apply to agriculture. "

Disproving Marxism "in instalments" could not satisfy Prof. Erik Nölting, a social-democrat and one of the most typical theoreticians of social-fascism. In one of his discourses entitled *What does Marxism mean to its to-day?* (reported in the *Frankfurter Volksstimme* of January 21st, 1928), he attempted to guillotine Marxism altogether.

He recapitulated his refutation of Marxism in ten points from which we can cull only a few excerpts:

1. Since Marx, capitalist society has changed in its basic structure . . . . The doctrine of crises is itself no longer tenable, as the crises of to-day have their origin in shocks that have arisen *outside the process of production*. . . .

2. As trade unions were formed, the labour market changed. . . . Marx taught that the worker must necessarily become impoverished, must sink lower and lower . . . . that his liberation would grow out of his destitution. But the most elevated sections are the basic troops of socialism. . . . Psychologically *the theory of pauperisation is erroneous*.

3. The peasant question remains entirely unsolved. Marx was a typical city dweller, an exile in flight. We assumed with him that the peasantry would travel the same path of concentration as the capitalists. . . . *That is a very grave misapprehension, etc.*

4. *The problem of socialisation as Marx saw it is too narrow.* In one place he wants social justice, then he wants the transfer of the means of production. . . . The socialisation proposal of Marx also lacks the concrete indication *as to whom* the means of production are to be transferred. *This we missed in the revolution.*

5. *The cultural question found no solution in orthodox Marxism.* . . . Marxism says that the proletarian stands in opposition to the bourgeois, hence his culture also stands in opposition to bourgeois culture. *Cultures did not grow out of the economic structure*, however much they were modified by it. The higher the proletarian rises the more the differences disappear. . . .

6. *International questions also found no exhaustive solution in Marxism.* The placard-like formula: "Proletarians of all countries, unite!" screens the actually existing differences between the workers of the individual nations.

7. *The democratic parliamentary state is a fact which can afford the proletariat the possibility of improving its position.* You must utilise this and not deny the State in the old Marxist sense. . . . Marx is of the opinion that the State is to be destroyed. But we see that it will only pass from one hand to the other. It is neither a purely bourgeois nor a purely proletarian matter. *In essence it is rather a matter of officials.* (Exactly the programme of the presidential government of von Papen and

108

von Schleicher. — B. K.).

8. The fact that there is an intermediate link between capitalism and socialism overcomes the Marxist conception of an explosive conversion from capitalism to socialism. This transitional phase finds threefold expression: (a) politically by coalition governments (Kautsky is the father of this idea. — B. K.); (b) economically by industrial democracy (Hilferding is the father of this idea. — B. K.); (c) socially through labour legislation (the paternity of this idea is difficult to establish, the entire international trade-union bureaucracy share the responsibility. — B. K.).

9. *Why the concept of determinism is superfluous.* Marxism is imbued with the belief that socialism must grow out of capitalism. Every movement seeks to base its *raison d'être* on hope in the determinism of its thesis.

Enough of this piffle of the most vulgar bourgeois science, which nevertheless, has one advantage in Prof. Nölting's recapitulation, *viz.*, that it contains almost everything that the leading theoreticians of the Second International have uttered at various times in refutation of Marxism. Marx passed judgment on such a garbled apology of capitalism, when in his preface to the first volume of *Capital* he wrote concerning these theoreticians that for them it is not a question

"Whether this or that theorem is true but whether it is useful or harmful, convenient or inconvenient for capitalism, whether allowed or not allowed by the police."

We could multiply *ad infinitum* such and similar declarations of social-democratic theoreticians and practitioners; in which Marx is "refuted," and forever "dethroned" They were especially numerous during the period of the relative stabilisation of capitalism when it seemed to them that Hilferding and Naphtali's "organised capitalism" had for ever rendered "unreal" the "irksome" law of capitalist production discovered by Marx and Engels. In the days of "prosperity," when it seemed to the social-democratic leaders that imperialism had overcome its post-war crisis, Marxism was thrown overboard as ballast by all parties of the Second International. Even its utilisation as a shibboleth to placate those who wanted to erect a bridge "between the past and the present of social-democracy" was reduced to a minimum.

But the period of shocks and jolts for industry and the end of relative stabilisation brought about by the accentuation of the world economic crisis in the capitalist countries, together with the simultaneous victorious advance of socialist construction in the Soviet Union (which it was impossible to conceal from the necessitous masses of the capitalist countries), the revolutionary upswing and the growing influx of the masses into the Communist Parties caused other winds to prevail. The practical as well as the theoretical victories of Marxism have compelled the enemies of Marxism to re-dress themselves in Marxian garb after all their seasonal theories have been torn to tatters.

After the election victory of the Communist Party of Germany on November 7th, two Marxian parties suddenly appeared in Germany on the horizon of the Vienna *Arbeiterzeitung*.

"Relatively the share of votes obtained by the *two Marxian* Parties has increased," wrote. Mr. Otto Bauer or one of his lieutenants after, the Reichstag elections in November, putting a pleasant face on an unpleasant situation.

The Berlin organ of the Social-Democratic Party, the *Vorwärts*, reprinted with special emphasis this new discovery of Otto Bauer's concerning the "two Marxist parties."

Mr. Vandervelde who, after the miners' strike in Borinage, had to record the fact that the reformistically organised Belgian workers were disinclined to follow the coalition policy of his party, wants to convince them in the name of "Marxism" that they ought to form a united front with the clericals instead of with the Communists. On the occasion of the last governmental crisis in Belgium he wrote in *Le Peuple* on December 11th:

"I am an *old Marxist*. I believe in the primacy of the economic factors. I am decidedly inimical to any reversion to political formulas that would push anti-clericalism again into the foreground. I would deprecate with all the power within me every action whose aim it would be to divide the working class still more against itself, by undertaking any attack whatever upon freedom of conscience and of instruction."

"Religion is opium for the people," wrote Marx. The chairman of the Second International is ready to falsely label himself an "old Marxist," so that the workers may believe him when he advocates a coalition with the dispensers of this opium.

The Social-Democrats, still Marxists only by the *grace of Hitler*, go so far that, at their party congress in Germany which is being called during the period of the Fiftieth Anniversary of the death of Karl Marx, Marx actually figures on their congress agenda. Rudolf Hilferding, author of *Finance Capital* and most devoted servant and avid beneficiary of finance capital, will make the introductory report at the party congress on " Marx and the Present Day." So it comes that Marxists by the grace of Hitler now lay "voluntary" *claim* to Marx.

We would like to recommend two slogans for the streamers that will decorate the congress hall when Hilferding delivers his address. Even without the use of clubs or beer jugs these two slogans would of themselves denote a battle in the meeting hall yet might be most appropriate on this occasion when Hilferding holds forth on Marx.

One of these slogans is by Marx himself: —

"*I am the mortal enemy of capitalism.*"

The promulgator of the other slogan was not a simple revolutionist like Marx; he demands that his honorary titles be enumerated: Ex-Chairman of the Social-Democratic Party of Germany, Member of the Council of People's Commissars in November, 1918, and First President of the German Republic. I refer to Friedrich Ebert. The watchword that is traceable to him and dates back to those same days of the November revolution reads:

"*I hate revolution like poison.*"

I entertain no hopes that this proposal of mine — although it would be a correct introduction to Hilferding's discourse on "Marx and the Present Day" — will be accepted. On the contrary, I think it is highly probable that Hilferding will solve this "slight discrepancy between the conceptions of Marx and Ebert in his own fashion which savours of Austro-Marxism — as follows:

"Well, you see, it's a matter of taste; this one hates capitalism, and that one revolution, but both were enamoured with Socialism!"

I think it is quite improbable that in his discourse Hilferding will deal with all questions that bear on his theme — especially such *current topics* as the development of social-democracy into social-fascism, its relation to fascism; the responsibility of the social democrats and the reformist trade unions for the lowering of the working-class standard of living; for the unemployment of millions.

These questions are of the utmost importance to the present-day labour movement. A correct reply to them can be made only by consulting Marx. This is the more necessary because many social-democratic workers feel offended if one speaks about their party as a social-fascist party and opine — *quite in good faith* — that the social-democratic party has retained something of Marxism. For this reason it is necessary to counterpose at least two important questions of the day; the relation of the social-democrats and the fascist's to the bourgeois State, and the wage policy of social-democracy and fascism, to the Marxist conception of the State and wage policy.

Let us next consider whether the *social-democratic conception of the State* which lies at the bottom of the "proposals for a united front," calling, as they do, upon the workers not only of Germany but of the entire world, to defend the Weimar Republic — whether this conception of the State, the expression of which is the Weimar Constitution, has anything in common with Marxism and whether there is any *essential* difference, any difference in principle, between it and the fascist conception of the State.

It is well known that Marxism represents the idea that the bourgeois State, and therefore the Weimar Republic also, is "the expression of the irreconcilability of class-contradictions," of the antagonism between the bourgeoisie and the proletariat, between capitalist and worker. The Weimar Constitution, its construction, cost the lives of tens of thousands of German proletarians, of their best leaders: *Liebknecht, Luxembourg, Jogiches* and others who were murdered by the myrmidons of Ebert, Noske and Wels in order to produce this Weimar Constitution with its Article 165 which lays it down that: —

"Workers and employees are to collaborate with the *entrepreneurs on an equal basis* in the regulation of the conditions of work and wages, as well as in the entire economic development of the *productive forces.*"

We see that this sentence in the Weimar Constitution, which was fought out in the *democratic counter-revolution against the proletarian revolution*, which the German worker is to defend according to the "proposals for a united front" made by Breitscheid, Kunstler, Otto Bauer, etc., has nothing in common with the Marxist conception of the "irreconcilability of class contradictions."

But this sentence in the Weimar Constitution corresponds so much the more — both in meaning and language — to the conception of the State entertained by the fascists.

Mussolini gives utterance to this principle upon which the social-democrats harp so much as his own principle in the following modest words

"We have incorporated all forces of production in the State. Labour and capital have *equal rights and equal duties*; they must work together, their conflicts being adjusted by recourse to law and the courts."

And the fascist constitutional charter in Italy, the "Carta del Lavoro" (Charter of Labour) contains the following article, corresponding to Article 165 of the Weimar Constitution:

"The trades corporations recognised by law guarantee *equality before the law* as between employers and employees. They maintain the discipline of *production* and promote its *perfection*."

Turati, the former General Secretary of the Fascist Party of Italy, could point with pride to its theories of communes expounded in the "Carta del Lavoro":

"The juridical recognition of the syndicates as organisations of public law, which are *authorised to represent all productive forces of the country* (the entrepreneurs and the workers by hand and brain), *forms the basic principle of the Fascist State*."

day, especially the *wage policy of the reformist trade unions*.

The wage policy of all trade unions which arc not to be designated as yellow but as organs of the class struggle, as organs for the defence of the daily interests of the working class — not to mention the struggle for the abolition of the wage system — was based upon the theory of Marx, according to which

"The general tendency of capitalist production is not to *raise* the average normal wage but to *lower it, i.e.*, to shift the value of labour more or less to its minimum" (Marx: *Value,*

Price and Profit).

Tarnow, the German trade union leader, joins issue with Marx here, giving it as his opinion that:

"The *individual* entrepreneur may figure now as before, that lowering wages can only be to his advantage. But for the entrepreneurs as a whole, this manipulation can no longer be practised without doing injury to the interests of capital and profit of the *entrepreneurs* themselves."

Marx was of the opinion that the workers must wage a struggle against the capitalists, varying in form, but *persistent*.

"The determination of the actual degree (*i.e.*, the degree of exploitation) is ascertained by the incessant struggle between capital and labour; the capitalist *constantly* tries to force down wages to their physically lowest and to draw out the working day to the physically longest, while the worker constantly exerts pressure in the opposite direction. The matter is solved by the question of the relative forces of the participants in the struggle" (*Value, Price and Profit*), — such is the other thesis upon which the Marxian trade union policy is founded.

Messrs. Nölting, whose text book *Introduction to Theoretical Economy* is considered a semiofficial publication of the A.D.G.B., entertain a different opinion:

"The formation of wages" — we read in this social-democratic text book — "is beyond the reach of strikes and the arbitrary will of parties. Every attempt to influence wages collapses by reason of its internal impossibility . . . . trade union wage policy, especially of the organisation and the carrying through of wage strikes is a fruitless and fateful illusion; laws can not be abrogated by *putsches*. A revolution against wages would be as nonsensical as a revolution against the law of gravitation."

It is difficult to imagine that anything in the works of the social-democratic theoreticians could possibly exhibit more open enmity against Marxism. None the less the following choice morsel comes from the pen of Naphtafi, whom Tarnow celebrated as the "Marx-substitute" of the reformist trade unions:

"To-day relations have changed essentially," this great discovery announces. "Legal relationships are being established between entrepreneurs and worker. To-day *we can no longer speak in general of exploitation of the workers by their employers.*"

These "refutations" of Marxism are the principles which form the basis of the policy of the A.D.G.B. This was the basis of its attitude on the question of capitalist rationalisation, when word was passed round that the "organisation" of capitalism was to be advanced at the expense of the working class by means of capitalist rationalisation. Everything that vulgar economy could invent was set up by the German trade union leaders in opposition to Marxism, was set in motion by the theoreticians of the German reformist trade unions to have the workers believe that what was being done under capitalism was in defence of their interests, actually promoted the realisation of their interests, much better than could be done by a socialism after the model of a "certain Marx." *Die Arbeit*, theoretical organ of the German trade unions, wrote at the time

"Every step in rationalisation is a lap on the way to the return to consumption economy, of course, big capitalist in form, but without big-capitalist spirit, and is consequently a big lump of socialisation. Thus a century-old dream is coming true."

Every word of which is so much bosh and nonsense! None the less, this omnium-gatherum of idiocies was the theoretical basis upon which the reformist trade union members were "voluntarily" subjected by their leaders to capitalist wage pressure in the halcyon days of capitalist rationalisation.

Time, however, brought changes in trade union tactics and a newer refutation of Marxism. Rationalisation could not even adduce the semblance of proof that the laws of capitalist production — discovered by Marx — had lost their validity. The "organisation" of capitalism could not master the crisis even with the aid of capitalist rationalisation. The theory according to which capitalism is interested in high wages was thus disproved. It was not the "individual entrepreneur" but the bourgeois State, the agent of the capitalist class or to use Tarnow's terminology — "of the entrepreneurs as a whole" which led the offensive against the wages of the working class. The industrial reserve army, the host of unemployed, grew to monstrous proportions during the crisis. Otto Bauer was immediately on the spot when a defence of social-fascist practice was to be *"theorised"* — the practice of the reformist trade unions which, by supporting the pressure upon wages, and because of the immense increase in unemployment, pressed the workers by supporting capitalist rationalisation, close to the border line of barbarism or even into barbarism itself. The new descriptive word of social-democracy for the defence of capitalist rationalisation was coined by Otto Bauer and is denominated *"mistaken rationalisation."*

The same Tarnow who conducted the chorus of the German trade union bureaucrats when they sang the praises of capitalist rationalisation had to admit publicly that "precipitate and overzealous rationalisation was one of the main causes of mass unemployment."

As the crisis sharpened the workers offered resistance to the capitalist offensive.

Marx's theory of trade union wage policy says clearly on this point that the working class should "utilise any occasional possibilities for temporary improvements . . . . If it were to yield in cowardly fashion in its daily conflicts with Capital, it would most assuredly deprive itself of the capacity to undertake any major movement."

But the question was precisely this: that the working class was to be restrained from utilising capitalism's critical state dine to the crisis, restrained from these "major movements," *i.e.*, from the proletarian revolution, from the struggle for socialism. That is why the entire social-democracy — supported by all sorts of renegades — proclaimed the theory: "No wage struggles, no strikes, during the crisis!"

The strike is, of course, far from being a revolution, but to underestimate the revolutionary significance of strikes is anything but Marxism. Both the social-democrats and the reformist trade union leaders correctly appraised the revolutionary significance of strikes — especially in times of crises — (more correctly than many Communists who do not understand the revolutionary significance of partial demands and partial struggles), by the supreme efforts they made, and are making, to hold the workers back from strikes in order thereby to be able to defend capitalism against proletarian revolution.

That is why Tarnow, the arch-reformist, advanced exactly the opposite kind of tactics against the trade-union tactics advocated by Marxism. In his notorious Königsberg discourse on the world economic crisis — delivered at a time when wage cuts were being handed out at high-pressure speed — Tarnow raised strike-breaking, instead of reforms and minor alleviations, to the rank of a theory.

"The crisis should not be regarded from the standpoint of the working class. The crisis must be tided over within the framework of capitalist economy by the sacrifices of the working class necessary for that purpose."

Now, whereas the trade-union theory and practice of social-democracy is the direct opposite of Marxian trade-union theory and practice, this theory of strike-breaking, enunciated by the social-fascists has all the traits *in common with the fascist point of view* as to the relation of the working class to the crisis and to wage movements. Small wonder, then, that while Tarnow was delivering himself of these astonishingly self-revealing sentiments, Hitler's personal press organ, the *Völkische Beobachter* was actually printing its stand on the matter in these words:

"if in this situation the economic demands of Germany's employees are examined from the point of view of right, it will be evident at first blush that reason is against them *because the entire economic scheme as such is on the verge of collapse.*"

Both declarations date back to November, 1930 — Tarnow's as well as that of Hitler's own paper.

Quite true, there have been few historical injustices to match the case of social-democracy which stands accused of Marxism for no reason whatever by its twin brother, fascism. The economic theory of social-fascism, the principles of which form the basis of the wage policy and the entire practice of the reformist trade unions, is as far distant from Marxism as it is close to the economic "theory" of national fascism.

The point of departure taken by the Marxist theory is that surplus value, which the employer appropriates in its entirety at the expense of the worker, has its origin in the *process of production.* From this fact follows the irreconcilable contradiction between the employer and the employee, the class contradiction between capitalist and wage worker. The point of departure of all vulgar economy, also of the economic "theory" of fascism is, on the contrary, *the process of exchange.* Profit springs not from the production of commodities but from their exchange.

But, according to the theories of both the fascists and social-fascists, harmony prevails in the process of production as between the interests of the capitalists and the wage workers.

This the programme of the N.S.D.A.P. (National Socialist Labour Party of Germany), expresses less scientifically than clearly by stating in its tenth paragraph:

"It must be the first duty of every citizen to do mental or physical work. The activity of the individual may not infringe upon the interests of the community, but must be pursued *within the framework of the entire body politic and must accrue to the advantage of all."*

Alfred Braunthal, one of the best-known economic theoreticians of social-democracy, propounds a theory in opposition to Marxism which is scientifically formulated, but whose content corresponds fully to the fascist programme. This theory is set forth in his *Present-Day Economy and its Laws*, and is intended for use as a text book. There this disciple of Otto Bauer says:

"The theory of productivity, viewed from the angle of wages, doubtless has practical significance and can be justified in one point, for the following law accords with it: Any rise in wages finds an absolute limit in the productivity of labour. And vice versa: the greater the productivity, the higher wages can, under certain circumstances, rise. In this respect *the theory of productivity is undoubtedly superior to the Marxist theory.*"

it is "superior" because it represents the interests of the capitalists by seeking to persuade the workers that an increase in the productivity of labour occurs "in the interests of the community" and "within the framework of the entire body politic and must accrue to the advantage of all" — to use the words of the fascist programme.

Braunthal's theory of wages strikes a different tune. There we are informed that:

"Of course not more can be divided than has been produced, and the more there is being produced, the more we have at our disposal for distribution. Therefore the worker is undoubtedly interested in the greatest possible increase in production. . . ." (Of course, everything Braunthal says has reference to the capitalist method of production. — B. K.).

While Braunthal bases the social-fascist theory of wages solely upon the harmony of interests between worker and employer in the capitalist process of production, Kautsky also found a different "reason" whereby the economic as well as the political struggle of the wage workers against the capitalists can

120

be regarded as the fascists regard it, namely, as an infringement upon the "interests of the community." In his preface to the popular edition of the second volume of *Capital*, Kautsky distorted this great work of Marx's *inter alia* by the following sentence:

"In the process of circulation phenomena arise which are of the greatest moment for the weal and woe of the workers and which do not lose in weight by the fact that here *workers and capitalists* have identical interests up to a certain degree."

"*Identical interests*" between workers and capitalists in the process of production as well as in the *process of circulation*. What else is there left? Against whom is the social-democratic worker to fight in the opinion of his theoreticians, his political and trade union leaders?

Nothing else remains but to fight against the workers who do not recognise these "identical interests between workers and capitalists," *against the Communists*, against the revolutionary proletarians who adhere to the Marxian doctrine — that the contradictions between Capital and Labour, bourgeoisie and proletariat, are not identical but irreconcilable.

So what does it mean when now a few social-democratic leaders like Otto Bauer, Vandervelde and company, in their immediate propinquity to fascism, suddenly make the discovery, under the blows of the crisis and the revolutionary upsurge, that somewhere in some country there are "two Marxian parties" — perhaps also two Marxian labour internationals? What significance attaches to this discovery after Kautsky's well-known statement that if what is going on in the Soviet Union — and what we all want to materialise throughout the world — is Marxism then his life had been in vain?

This discovery is nothing more or less than an attempt to parry the *main blow* of the revolutionary proletariat which, in the struggle for socialism, must necessarily be directed against the internal foe of the proletariat, against the social-democracy.

The Otto Bauers,

"the people who," as Marx and Engels wrote concerning such types in the labour movement, "under the guise of incessant hustle and bustle, not only do nothing themselves, but even endeavour to hinder others so that nothing but idle chatter results . . . these self-same people who see a reaction (which they help into the saddle. — B. K.), and then are perfectly astonished to find themselves in an impasse where neither resistance nor flight avail, the same people who want to cram history into their narrow philistine horizon and whom history passes by each time without taking note of them,"

these people, caught in a deadlock, now write concerning the unity which they have split. They vociferate about the defence of the interests of the workers whom they have sold and sell every day of the year. They inveigh against the "nonsense of the Communists" who direct their main blow against the newly-discovered "Marxian party." All their clamour about unity is because they know that in the difficult times of this crisis, of preparation for imperialist war, of military intervention against the Soviet Union, the proletariat presses for *unity of action.*

The sort of united front the social-democrats, who raise the hue and cry against the Communists, want is exemplified by the conference of the leaders of the national committee of German youth organisations which met on November 26th at which all tendencies were represented, social-democrats as well as national-socialists, with the sole exception of the Communist youth. This conference, which had "Youth in the Struggle for Germany" on its agenda, is reported in the *Gewerkschaftszeitung* (Trade organ of the A.D.G.B., in an in panegyrics, as stating that:

"*For the trade unions* it was interesting to see that among the numerous groups represented at the conference of the Reich committee of the German youth organisations none could be found to sponsor a policy of *laissez-faire.* It is also noteworthy that in the concluding remarks by Prof. Flitner, as well as in various Press comments, the question was raised whether it was not time for the leaders of the youth organisations to endeavour *to take a common and positive stand on concrete questions of the day.*"

Naturally, the organ of the A.D.G.B. is in favour of a "common and positive stand on concrete questions of the day" between the social-democratic and the fascist youth. For where there is no essential difference of opinion in the main question of to-day: defence of capitalism or the shattering of capitalism, such a common attitude is not at all difficult to maintain.

There have been cases where the social-democrats have succeeded — in the interests of capitalism — in perverting the pressure of the proletariat for *unity of action* into a *unity farce*. There are still many proletarians, I am certain, who — under the influence of social-democracy and the reformist trade unions — still flail to differentiate between unity of action in the class struggle, and the unity farce that serves the interests of the bourgeoisie.

In an unpublished letter of Engels' we find a splendid reply to Otto Bauer's hypocritical jeremiads concerning the "nonsense of the Communists" who direct the main blow against the social-democrats, who want to realise the united front of the Communist and social-democratic, of the organised and the unorganised workers, but who are disinclined to enter into a "united front" with the misleaders of the social-democratic workers — with the leaders of the Second and the Amsterdam Internationals and their sections, whose bankrupt policy was characterised as follows by the *Arbeiter Zeitung* of October 9th, 1932:

"The German workers have sacrificed themselves for the State, have again and again placed their own interests after those of the State. The German bourgeoisie is thankful to them for this — through Hitler and Papen."

123

In this letter from Engels to Bebel, dated January 20th, 1886, we find the following:

"In France the long-expected split has become a fact. The original rapprochement between Guesde and Lafargue, and Melon and Brousse could not be avoided, I suppose, on founding the party, but neither Marx nor I ever laboured under any illusions about the fact that this could not endure. The point in dispute is purely one of principle: whether *the struggle* is to be conducted *as a class struggle* of the proletariat against the bourgeoisie, or is it to be permitted in good opportunist fashion (or to translate it into socialist languageJpossibilist fashion) to drop the class character of the movement and the programme wherever more votes, more followers, can be gained by doing so. . . . The development of the proletariat is everywhere the result of internal struggles, and France, which now is forming a Workers' Party for the first time, is no exception. We in Germany are beyond the first phase of the internal struggle. Other struggles are still ahead of us. Unity is all right as long as it lasts, but some things take precedence over unity. And when one has fought all one's life more than anyone else against self-styled socialists, as Marx and I have done (for the bourgeoisie we tackled only as a class and almost never engaged in single combat with one cannot lose any tears over the inevitable struggle has the bourgeois) the fact that broken out."

This is the corroboratory judgment of and Engels concerning the theory that the blow of the revolutionary masses in the struggle against the main enemy, the bourgeoisie — must be directed against social-democracy. This is the answer Marx and Engels have for political bankrupts who desire to manoeuvre their way out of the deadlock at the expense of the workers they have betrayed. This is the keynote for our activities to effect a real united front of the working class, a united front from below, in the daily struggles which must be led on to the decisive struggles for power.

IV.

The insurrection of the forces of production against private property in the means of production, against the capitalist production relationships which are the life springs of the bourgeoisie and its domination, has won greater vigour by the economically and politically decisive fact that the Union of Socialist Soviet Republics exists and is victorious, while the capitalist world has approached the point where the *dynamiting of Marx main the capitalist relations of production* commences. Never before has the bourgeoisie proved itself so clearly a "superfluous class" as now. In its own countries it contemplates the crisis with despair as it breaks out with ever-renewed fury. It founds its domination more and more upon open terror against its wage slaves, whose millions lack the absolute minimum of existence.

But in the country where *Socialism has become a fact*, in the Soviet Union, it is daily proven that the working class, freed from its exploiters and oppressors, now its own master and ruling in its own right in the Soviets, develops the socialised forces of production at a tempo that staggers imagination, while at the same time appropriating socially the social product of labour. By abolishing the conditions of life under which it lived in bourgeois society, it abolishes "*all* the inhuman conditions of life" that capitalism has created: no unemployment, abolition of the slavery of woman, abolition of the oppression of more than a hundred nationalities. The general crisis of the capitalist system means also a crisis for the *material power* of society, the power of the ruling class, especially in view of the simultaneous triumphal march of socialism in the Soviet Union. This crisis for the material power evokes at the same time a crisis of the ruling *intellectual power*, of the prevailing bourgeois ideology.

The capitalist system which cannot give bread nor work to tens of millions of its wage slaves can also no longer cover their intellectual needs with its ideologies, not even with "anticapitalist ideology," can no longer *constantly* satisfy them.

125

The period of the intensification of the general economic crisis is at the same time a period of crisis of all bourgeois ideologies which also figure as a means whereby the bourgeoisie may keep exploited and oppressed masses in check. The hunger of the masses, especially of the millions of young workers whose "graduation to life" takes place at a time of severest deprivations, of unemployment and terror, demands not only work and bread, but also a *world outlook*. The period of the general crisis has become the period of "grave doubts" on the part of the bourgeoisie. Words like dislocation, disintegration, internecine struggle, cataclysm, ruin and chaos are now in very common usage not only in the sphere of science but also of ideology.

"What is the point at issue?" queries someone active in fascist circles who arrogates to himself the rôle of ideologist of *young Germany*. "That is the decisive question which everyone who thinks at all must ponder, which gives him no peace and agitates his entire being. Is that which we are living through today the result and the aim of a development which has devoured untold sacrifice and which has shaken man from head to foot? Is this the end?"

But also in the *victor countries*, in France, in England, in the United States, the words written by Hegel in his *Philosophy of History* concerning the wars of Napoleon are more than applicable to their economy as well as to their ideology:

"No greater victories have ever been gained, no more genial moves have ever been made; but likewise the *impotence of victory* never appeared in a more striking light."

The nationalism rampant in the countries of victor and vanquished alike is an *expression of the impotence* that has seized the world after the repartition of the world by the Versailles Peace Treaty and the Washington Convention had tenfold increased the number of potential startingpoints of war to-day. On the other hand, it is also the consequence of the impotence of the bourgeoisie in the province of home policy, an expression of the fact, that as a result of the crisis, it feels itself more and more constricted in the application of its ideology of social reforms and is constrained to have recourse almost exclusively to what is the sheerest national damagogy.

Pacifism — that falsification of the honest will of the workers to peace, first omen of instinctive protest against imperialist war and of the awareness of a reactionary character in the clandestine preparations of imperialist war and military intervention against the Soviet Union is undergoing a profound crisis. The bourgeoisie becomes less and less capable of concealing the fact that the cause of war lies in imperialist capitalism itself; that *capitalism and war are inseparable*. Those who used to be pacifists by honest conviction are experiencing a change of heart. They are forsaking pacifism and drawing nearer to the idea of revolutionary struggle against capitalism as the cause of war. This was one lesson taught by the Amsterdam Anti-War Congress. Those, on the other hand, who were not the deceived but the deceivers in the pacifist movements are now revealing themselves more and more to the masses as the pacifist agents in this work of preparation for imperialist war and intervention.

The "revalorisation of all values," that expression of disbelief in all traditional ideologies which always tends to crop up among the bourgeoisie in all crises of capitalism, extends to all spheres of bourgeois ideology, but more especially to the problem of the possibility of survival for the capitalist system itself.

Those political and economic leaders, leading ideologists of the bourgeoisie, who still entertain the belief that capitalism can continue as of old, are "white ravens" indeed. The words of the bourgeois, as well as social-democratic economic healers of the bourgeoisie concerning "late-capitalism" and "organised capitalism," only seek to veil the hideous fact that for them capitalism has come to the end of its tether and that of course an attempt must be made to save it somehow. Optimists are scarce. But their optimism is no less impotent than the gloomy forebodings of the pessimists.

"The danger that man will become the slave of his tool," wrote Prof. Adolf Weber, one of the optimistic champions of capitalism after the crisis had set in, "cannot be averted by changing the economic system, but only by influencing the patterns of thought and soul-life of man."

The accentuated crisis of capitalist economy surely greets this inane prattle with derisive laughter. For it "freed" forty to fifty million proletarians, who had become unemployed, from the "slavery of their tools." It never even permitted the millions of youth to reach the status of "slaves of their tools." "Influence upon the patterns of thought and the soul-life of man" — that is social-democracy; that is fascism. *How long they will suffice* to stem the rising tide of the proletariat beating against the capitalist system, against the bourgeoisie, is to-day the greatest worry of the capitalists and their ideology manufacturers.

In this period of "grave doubt," of the "revalorisation of all values," when everything in economy, in the machinery of power, in the ideology of capitalism, has been shaken to its deepest foundations, the edifice of Marxian doctrine stands firm and proud in all its parts and particles, untouched by the crisis of ideologies.

Prof. Schmalenbaeh, a most prominent bourgeois theoretician of industrial economy, has said with resignation:

"What difference is there in essence between what we are going through to-day and the fulfilment of the predictions made by Marx, the great socialist?"

Nor is it this "recognition" of Marx on the part of an ideologist of the bourgeoisie that most glaringly characterises the discomfiture of bourgeois ideology and its defeat by Marxism-Leninism. The following is perhaps less self-evident but none the less much more characteristic: *the turning of the*

128

bourgeoisie, in its period of decline, *away from* everything it had created during its *period of ascent*. Marx and Engels — however much their theory was "rooted in the material economic facts" — in the theoretical elaboration of scientific socialism, derived their start from the best that the young bourgeoisie had created in its period of ascent in the realm of ideology, that being "the thought material on hand."

This "thought material on hand" was supplied by *German classical philosophy* — primarily *Hegel, English classical political economy*, primarily *Smith* and *Ricardo*, and *French socialism*, primarily *Saint Simon* and *Fourier.* The elabortion of *scientific socialism*, of *Communism*, by Marx and Engels, proceeded theoretically in the form of a *critique* of these doctrines, *i.e.*, by contrasting these doctrines with the objective facts and their coherence. All that transcended in these systems the limited borders of bourgeois thinking was rescued by Marx and Engels and given over to the proletariat.

The putrescent bourgeoisie in the period of its decline repudiates even the remnants of those intellectual products produced in the heyday of its development as a class.

Hugo Schulz, a bourgeois economist, recently confessed that the bourgeoisie had to abandon *the classical theory of political economy* as it could not combat Marxism from the standpoint of this theory. The period of the present crisis is the period of a revival of vulgar economy in the camp of bourgeois science to an extent never witnessed before. A refutation of *all law* in economy, and the rejection of every theory, is the main trait of these hirelings of bourgeois economy. For them the economic crisis is not a consequence of the regular economic development, its cause does not lie "in economy" but "in the soul"; it is a "crisis of confidence." Vulgar economics like this have nothing in common with the classical theory of political economy which the best representatives of the young bourgeoisie elaborated in the struggle against feudalism that the capitalist method of production might be victorious.

German classical philosophy, which translated the great French revolution into the field of philosophy for the cowardly German bourgeoisie, is to-day as dead as a door nail as far as it (the German bourgeoisie) is concerned. Hegel, greatest representative of the classical school, is again singled out by the bourgeoisie for treatment as a "dead dog." Marx and Engels linked up the dialectic method with the revolutionary side of Hegelian philosophy. They stripped dialectics of their mystical covering of Hegelian idealism. They turned dialectics "up-side down" by demonstrating that the "ideal" is nothing else than the "material" converted and translated in the mind of man.

The bourgeoisie in the period of its crisis had to repudiate Hegel since his dialectics were intolerable for it even in their idealistic covering. Hegelian dialectics preclude precisely that which is most necessary for the idealogists of the bourgeoisie in the course of the crisis: *the contemplation of the existing, of the existing order of society, as something endowed with finality.*

Flight from truth, flight into the "intellectual," is a general phenomenon in bourgeois science. The one takes refuge in religion — not only Christian religions, but also the ancient heathen religions, as certain fascist tendencies in Germany do, in oriental religions, in Buddhism, like the English theosophists. Within the bourgeoisie multifarious schools of philosophical mysticism prosper. It is the religion of the refined bourgeoisie, which has lost faith in the Christian as well as in the Jewish god, inasmuch as the Jewish god in his unity and the Christian god in all his trinity have proved themselves incapable of preserving capitalism from the crisis.

Not even the youth is spared this flight from the truth. The youth movement which finds expression in the "back to nature" ideologies: the cult of the old Germanic; of the Celtic, all sorts of vegetarian sects, religious pacifism, etc., are nothing but disintegrated products of bourgeois ideology.

Social-democracy too takes flight "into the intellectual."

The English trade union bureaucrats and American Socialist leaders unite their bureauaratmc functions in the labour organisations with the post of preachers in various ecclesiastical sects. Religious socialists find more favour in the social-democratic parties than radical free-thinkers. Sollmann, a German social-democratic leader, professes positive Catholicism. Otto Bauer has become nothing less than a god-seeker who has elevated a timeless, spaceless, and classless "freedom of conscience" to be his social-democratic god. The worst kinds of inane idealism have replaced the old French materialism and even the idealism of classical German philosophy.

In France the various radical-socialist tendencies — which in a certain sense consider themselves *heirs of the French Revolution and French socialism* — have discarded all semblance of kinship with the great utopians of French socialism and the great French Revolution. The socialism of the great utopians sallied forth from the traditions of the French Revolution to the watchwords: *liberty, equality, fraternity.* For these watchwords the radical-socialist groups in France have substituted the trinity: *Panama-scandal-corruption.*

To-day more than ever it is appropriate, is the high duty of every Communist, of every young Communist worker, to bear aloft the flag of Marxism-Leninism, the revolutionary "doctrine of the conditions of victory the working class;" to make Marxism-Leninism the common property of all proletarians seeking a world philosophy and emancipation. This duty now becomes paramount in the period of "grave doubt," which has penetrated even the ranks of the proletarian youth.

Special significance attaches to-day to Lenin's words: "Without revolutionary theory there can be no revolutionary movement." Millions of youth — without any trade or profession, millions of adults who are losing their professional training through unemployment, who have been thrown upon the street, are now in quest not only of "room to live" but also of a "principle of life," of a guide to action that will enable them to win for themselves "room to live." They need a revolutionary theory to be able to resist the seduction of fascist demagogy, of social-democratic hypocrisy.

The bourgeoisie not only holds on to its positions in the process of production; retains its hold on capitalist private property with all possible tenacity, with all the power of its material force up to and even after its overthrow, but also insists upon the propagation of its ideology no matter how low it is laid by the crisis. It does this the more in view of the fact that this ideology also represents a measure of power which helps it to maintain its shaken domination.

Fascism it is which, as a method of government having recourse openly to armed force, to terror, and as an ideology which is being applied wherever and whenever social-democracy alone is not adequate to act as intermediary in bringing bourgeois influence into the working class to keep the indignant proletariat in check, is the expression of this tenacious, desperate *life-and-death* struggle of capitalism *for its domination*, for its very existence.

To free the workers won by fascism, especially the young workers, from the ideology of despair that drove them to fascism is possible only in a persevering struggle conducted with the weapons of Marxist-Leninist theory. This, of course, refers no less to the masses of workers and young workers which directly or indirectly, under the influence of social-democracy, are unwilling props in the main support of bourgeois dictatorship. The superiority of Marxism-Leninism as the consciousness of the working class over fascism and social-fascism cannot be doubted. Here the question is, on the one hand, only this: that our practice in the political-economic struggle has not been sufficiently pervaded by this theory; on the other hand, that our theoretical struggle lags far behind the requirements necessary to destroy the ideological-political influence of social-democracy and fascism in the working class.

Let us be honest with ourselves, comrades. Let each one take stock of himself and confess how often he remembers that the historical struggle of the proletariat does not proceed only in two forms of struggle. How often are we mindful of what Engels wrote and what Lenin and Stalin always emphasised — that the historical struggle for the liberation of the proletariat must proceed not only in two forms, in the form of the political and economic struggle, but in three forms: in the form of the political, economic and theoretical struggle, if the proletariat is to attain victory.

I have no doubt but that especially the neglect of the economic front of the class struggle, the boycotting of trade union work on the part of many revolutionists which is customary in the Communist Parties — to-day rather covert but none the less existent — is the consequence of the inadequate theoretical insight into the conditions and methods of the revolutionary class struggle, the consequence of the lack of knowledge of Marxist-Leninist theory.

I now put another question, comrades: How often are we mindful of the facts recorded by Engels back in 1875, the beginning of the socialist mass movement, when he stated that:

"Indifference to all theory . . . . is one of the main causes responsible for the fact that the English labour movement, despite all the excellent organisations of its individual apparatus, creeps along at such a snail's pace; and on the other hand, for the mischief and confusion which Proudhonism in its original form wrought among the French and the Belgians, and in a form more caricatured by Bakunin among the Spaniards and Italians."

Translate this, English, French, Spanish and Italian comrades, into the language of the present-day movement in your respective countries. Think of the narrow "practicism" of the leaders of the English trade unions and of the Labour Party who "reject all theory." In order to be able under this guise the more easily to smuggle all kinds of bourgeois and petty-bourgeois theories such as the theory of industrial peace and of guild socialism into the working class. Think of French syndicalism which exhibits many essential reactionary traces of petty-bourgeois Proudhonist anarchism; think of the reformist syndicalists, of the Minoritaries within and without the C.G.T.L.! Think of the *Spanish anarcho-syndicalists* who were and are the props of bourgeois counter-revolution in Spain and who with their caricature revolutionism mislead many good revolutionary workers and keep them back from the struggle for the advancing of the bourgeois democratic revolution into the stage of proletarian revolution.

And you, young Communists of Germany! Remember what Engels wrote concerning the German working class in whose ranks Marx fought his first battles:

"The German workers must be given credit for the fact that they exploited the advantage of their situation (as the birthplace of Marxism — B. K.) with rare ingenuity. For the first time since a labour movement has been in existence is the struggle being conducted harmoniously, co-ordinatedly and planfully on all its three fronts, the theoretical, the political and the practical-economic (resistance against the capitalists). Precisely in this what may be called *concentrated* attack lies the strength and invincibility of the German movement."

Remember that in your victories also this *good* tradition of the German labour movement is and will continue to be effective; but reflect also whether the degree of concentration of the struggle to-day does not leave much to be desired in many instances.

No doubt the fact that we have been unable to enlarge our *mass influence* at the expense of Social-Democracy in all countries, of the anarcho-syndicalists in Spain and South America, of the reformist trade union leaders in the entire world, to the extent that this may have been possible in the given objective situation, is largely due to our failure to conduct our *agitational and propaganda work* among the masses sufficiently on principle, with an adequate Marxist-Leninist basis. To-day when everything — the crisis, the revolutionary upsurge, the end of capitalist stabilisation, the *great fundamental questions, questions of principle, of* the struggle for and the way to socialism, the question Dictatorship or Democracy? when the victories of socialist construction in the Soviet Union — places the question of classless society now confronting the broad masses of the workers inevitably upon the order of the day, this is *an especially grave shortcoming in our mass work*. The point is that Social-Democracy, because of the trouncing it is receiving at the hands of the revolutionary working masses in the capitalist countries, feels compelled to act as if it wanted to return to a "policy of principle." The "Left" manœuvres denote a broader exploitation of pseudo Marxian phraseology. These attempts to mislead the workers through these pseudo-Marxist phrases can be combatted successfully only by unfolding a thorough *propaganda of Marxism-Leninism* and by *basing our day-to-day policy on a broad footing upon basic principles*. Likewise dryness, pedanticism, bureaucracy, these poisonous weeds that often take root in our mass work and which youth can bear least — these too can be fought with no better means than by imbuing our day-to-day work with the *revolutionary spirit and ardour of Marxism-Leninism*.

Nor let us forget the *problem of cadres*, a question that is in as bad shape as our mass work. How can we burrow deep enough if in dealing with this question we do not act on the directions given by Engels:

"It is the duty of the leaders to enlighten themselves more and more on all theoretical questions, to free themselves more and more from the influence of traditional phrases appertaining to the old world philosophy and ever to bear in mind that socialism since it has become a science must needs be treated like one, *i.e.*, be studied. The point will be to disseminate with steadily mounting zeal among the workers the increasingly clarified discernment thus gained, to weld the

135

organisations of the Party as well as of the trade union associations ever closer together."

Who can assert that the "influence of traditional phrases appertaining to the old world philosophy" — above all Social-Democratic conceptions in the Communist Parties as well as in the sections of the Young Communist International — is nonexistent and does not act as a stumbling block an our way *to conquer the majoriy of the working class*? One should not seek comfort in the belief that youth has no Social-Democratic traditions like their elders. Unfortunately the fact is that neither age nor youth guard against folly. Social-Democratic conceptions percolate into the Communist movement not only via custom and traditions. The strenuous efforts of the petty-bourgeoisie seeking to maintain its existence finds expression also in the ideological pressure which this moribund medial stratum of society (incapable itself of conducting any independent policy), steadily exerts upon the working class. The strength of the labour aristocracy consists not so much in its numbers as in its key position in production — especially to-day in the period of the crisis — and it is precisely this position which is utilised as a conduit to pump bourgeois ideology into the broad masses of the workers. *Social-Democracy* is nothing more or less than *the bourgeois poison* that is innoculated through the petty-bourgeoisie, through the labour aristocracy, *day by day* into the heads of the workers. *The sole and exclusive antidote in the Marxist-Leninist enlightenment of the workers through cadres trained for that purpose*. It would be a denial of Marxism-Leninism, which is the revolutionary consciousness of the working class, an anti-Bolshevik deference to spontaneity, to think that without a thorough Marxist-Leninist education the officials of our Party and youth organisation can be made into leading *Bolshevik cadres* free from petty-bourgeois social-democratic inhibitions, into cadres that understand politics — the art of figuring with millions, the art of leading millions — who, in *the coming war* will do their bit without any hesitancy, who can *lead the proletariat to victory*!

Look at the Party of the Bolsheviks, hardened and steeled in three revolutions, in civil wars and last but not least in splits and in the struggle for the erection of the united front of the working class! This Party learnt the art of conquering in the political and economic struggle by never neglecting the theoretical struggle, by making splendid use of the burnished weapons of Marxist theory in the struggle against the Mensheviks as well as the "Left" currents.

Consider our two greatest and most victorious leaders: Lenin, the greatest theoretician and tactician of the proletarian revolution and the dictatorship of the proletariat — and the perpetuator of his work, Stalin, the theoretician and tactician of socialist construction. It was and is their greatest source of strength, and at the same time their greatest pride, that they were and are the best disciples of Marx and Engels who devoted a major portion of their knowledge and their revolutionary fighting energy to the struggle on the theoretical front, to the defence of Marxism-Leninism against every counterfeit.

Proud and eager for battle we claim:

Marx is ours!

But we must *take possession* of him if we are to be accoutred for battle and victorious.

We must permit the broad masses of adult and young workers *to share this possession* of ours, so that they may he transformed into conscious fighters for the cause of the liberation of the working class and into conscious builders of socialism through the dictatorship of the proletariat.

East and West, North and South, the proletarian millions rally to the red banner of the Communist International of Marx, Engels and Lenin! From the tops of the industrial titans of the Soviet Union the five beams of light radiating from the Soviet star illumine the path to be trod by the proletarians and oppressed peoples of all five continents, who crave and fight for *bread, work and liberation*. The capitalist system, the power of

137

the exploiters and oppressors, the power of the imperialist bourgeoisie, rocks to its very foundations. The more we strain our every effort to see to it that Marxist *theory*, penetrates the masses, the more this theory becomes the *force* that will deal the *death blow* to the power of the bourgeoisie!

The time has come for the proletariat to carry out this world-liberating deed in pursuance of its historical mission discovered by Marx: *it is now*!

Let the petty bourgeois denizens, the pedants, the philistines, the counterfeiters of Marxism, the traitors to the working class, the murderers of its best leaders and fighters shriek to their hearts' content about the "dislocation, ruin and chaos" which it is claimed the revolution will call forth — the proletariat, flying the flags of the Communist International, will pursue its road plotted by Marx and Engels and graded by Lenin and Stalin. The call then is forward along the road of struggle for the socialist revolution, for the dictatorship of the proletariat, for the victory of communism throughout the world!

The Most Burning Question: Unity of Action

FOREWORD

For over a year and a half Adolf Hitler, chief of the German fascists, has been wading in blood. The incendiaries of the Reichstag, Hitler, Goering, Goebbels and the rest, are trying to instigate a new imperialist war. The military-fascist clique of generals and admirals in Japan is holding its army and navy ready and waiting on the eastern borders of the Soviet Union. The international political situation may be subject to great variations, but one fact remains certain: Every imperialist country is already preparing for an imperialist war.

Fascism has become the principal instrument in these preparations for a new war. The offensive of capital on the living standard of the working class is designed to cover the costs of armaments. By robbing the working class of its rights and breaking up its organizations, the capitalists want to throttle the resistance of the working class against wars and robbery.

Working Class Ranks Split

In the face of this threatening new catastrophe, the ranks of the working class have been split since 1914. Unity is a crying need. Only the unity of the working class against the instigators of war, against fascist oppressors, against the source of imperialist wars and of fascism — capitalism — can alter the relation of class forces in favor of the proletariat.

The Communist Parties in all capitalist countries are waging a dauntless struggle to restore the unity of action of the working class, this being the necessary condition for drawing over the middle strata in town and country to the side of the proletariat. The Communist Parties have also addressed themselves to the leaders of the Social-Democratic Parties in

139

order to achieve the united front of the working class. The results as yet are insignificant. Only in France, in Austria, and in the Saar region have agreements been come to between Communist and Social Democratic workers. The difficulties are still great, but they are not insuperable.

Destroy Class Collaboration

However great these difficulties may be, the Communist Parties will dauntlessly continue their struggle against fascism and imperialist war, against the offensive of capital. The rejection of united front proposals by a number of Social-Democratic Parties may make this struggle more difficult, but it can never hold it up. Class collaboration with the bourgeoisie is the obstacle in the way of establishing unity of action. The natural condition for establishing the unity of action of the working class is to break the class collaboration with the capitalists. This does not mean that the contradictions — in tactics and in matters of principle — between Communism and Social-Democracy will be done away with. Nevertheless, the common struggle of Social-Democratic and Communist workers in the factories, in the trade unions, among both employed and unemployed, is the first prerequisite for overcoming the split in the ranks of the working class.

No one who is against the splitting of the proletariat, no one who wants the liberation of the working class, can refuse this common struggle against the dangers with which the working class is directly threatened.

The Communists, who are leading the liberation struggle of the working class, who, for this very reason reject all collaboration with the bourgeoisie, will continue to fight for unity of action. The success of this struggle depends first and foremost upon the Social-Democratic workers. They must decide: Either with the bourgeoisie against the members of their own class, or with their own class comrades against the bourgeoisie.

140

These articles, written at various stages of this struggle, are designed, by way of persuasion, to help the Social-Democratic workers to make this decision.

The working class, which fights unitedly and irreconcilably against the bourgeoisie, is invincible; it will conquer.

Bela Kun
Moscow, July 28, 1934

THE MOST BURNING QUESTION—UNITY OF ACTION

(Member of the Presidium of the Executive Committee of the Communist International)

Three Communist Parties have recently addressed themselves to three Social-Democratic Parties with the proposal for joint action in order to rescue the leader of the German Proletariat, Comrade Ernst Thaelmann, from the hands of the fascist hangmen. The fight to save Thaelmann is the fight for the release of all anti-fascist fighters in Germany, in Austria, and in all countries where fascism has been victorious. The Communists have never hesitated for an instant when it was a question of defending the lives of anti-fascist fighters who were in the ranks of Austrian Social-Democracy, or who, though not adhering to any party, carried on the struggle against the oppression of the working class.

The Central Committee of the Communist Party of France addressed a proposal to the Administrative Commission of the Socialist Party of France to organize joint demonstrations in a number of important industrial centers in France, especially in those cities where the Hitler government has its official

141

representatives.

Swiss C.P. Proposed Unity

The Central Committee of the Communist Party of Switzerland likewise sent a delegation to the chairman of the Swiss Socialist Party with the proposal to organize joint demonstrations against German fascism and for the rescue of Thaelmann.

The Central Committee of the Communist Party of Great Britain made similar addresses to the Labor Party, to the leaders of the reformist trade unions and co-operatives.

In personal negotiations between representatives of the French Socialist Party and the Communist Party of France, the Social-Democratic delegates declared themselves ready to agree to the proposal of the Communists on the condition that during the period of joint action, the Communist Party of France should refrain from all polemics against Social-Democracy. The delegates of the Communist Party of France declared that they were ready to cease all criticism of Social-Democracy during the period of joint action in those places where the demonstrations were to take place.

Swiss Socialists Reject Proposals

The Administrative Commission of the Socialist Party of Switzerland rejected the proposal of the Communist Party of Switzerland in a malicious answer of which we will quote only one sentence:

"If the Communist Party of Switzerland invites us to take part in demonstrations before the German embassies, we challenge the Communist Party of Switzerland to demonstrate before the RUSSIAN EMBASSIES in those countries where it is still able to do so."

Comment on this proposal is superfluous.

The leaders of the Labor Party have up to the present time (June 15, 1934), not yet answered the proposal sent them by the secretary of the Communist Party of Great Britain.

Such are the facts.

Bourgeoisie Fears United Front

To these facts we will only add one or two observations: The bourgeoisie, especially the German fascists, correctly estimate the importance of the unity of action of the working class as being the greatest danger for capitalism. They likewise correctly estimate the importance of the person of Comrade Thaelmann and of his defense in the anti-fascist struggle. In connection with the proposals made by the Communist Party of France to French Social-Democracy, the Berliner Boersenzeitung, one of the leading organs of big German capital, wrote as follows:

"We cannot, however, regard with indifference the fact that the French Communists are now preparing great meetings and street demonstrations in Paris, Reims, Lille, Strassbourg, Bordeaux, Marseilles and other cities for the rescue of Thaelmann, and have even contrived to induce French Social-Democracy to take part in these actions and to form a united front."

It is with good reason that this fascist paper agitates against the united front of Communist and Social-Democratic workers; it does so in the interests of German fascism and in the interests of capitalism as a whole.

This reaction on the part of Hitler fascism to the united front of the workers, which is developing against German fascism, is in itself enough to show that the Communist Parties which made proposals for unity of action to the Social-Democratic Parties acted correctly. The correctness of this step of the Communist Parties lies not only in the fact that they have repeated this step, despite the fact that after Hitler's advent to

143

power, the Second International forbade the Social-Democratic Parties to organize joint actions with the Communists against Hitler fascism. (The Second International did this despite the fact that the Communist International in its appeal of March 5, 1933, recommended its sections to cease making attacks on Social-Democracy during the period of joint actions.)

Moreover, the importance of these proposals made by the Communist Parties to the leaders of Social-Democratic Parties lies not only in the fact that Swiss Social-Democracy has once again proved that it prefers to maintain its class collaboration with the bourgeoisie rather than to establish the united front with the Communist workers; that the Labor Party could not even answer the proposal for unity of action made to it; that the French Socialists made joint action against fascism dependent upon a condition which constitutes a breach of workers' democracy.

C. P. Will Press Unity

At the time of writing these lines, we do not yet know what decision will be taken by the Administrative Commission of the French Socialist Party on the basis of the reports of its delegates who negotiated with the representatives of the Communist Party. We do not know which pressure will have a more powerful effect upon the Administrative Commission — the militant will of the working masses who are pressing for unity of action, or the resistance of Frossard, Doroy and Reviere, who have rejected the proposal made by the Communist Party of France. No matter what the leaders of French Social-Democracy may decide, no matter what the leaders of the Swiss Social-Democracy have decided, no matter what the leaders of the Labor Party have kept quiet from their members the Communist Parties will unshakably continue and extend the struggle for the united front of the working class against fascism, against war, for the rescue of Thaelmann.

Let the Social-Democratic leaders answer the proposals

of the Communists for the formation of a joint front of struggle with such malicious words as were used by Swiss Social-Democracy; let them declare with malice and hatred that the struggle against the splitting of the working class is a Communist maneuver — for us Communists, and also, we hope, for the great mass of workers in Social-Democratic and reformist organizations, the united front of the working class, the unity of action of the proletarians, is and remains a serious matter, a sacred cause.

Strongest Champions of Cause

Little as we Communists are inclined to surrender for one instant the political and organizational independence of the Communist Parties, little as we deem it possible for there to be a union of the Communist International with the Second International, we are nevertheless determined to fight with all our strength to secure the unity of action of the proletariat against its class enemies. Many Social-Democratic workers, members of reformist trade unions and functionaries of these organizations did not understand this before; but today at least, in face of the tremendous growth of the danger of fascism and war, they are coming to realize ever more and more clearly that the Communists are not an obstacle in the way of establishing the unity of the working class, but that they are the strongest champions of this cause.

The appeal for common action against fascism and the offensive of capital issued by the Communist International on March 5, 1933, had already convinced many of the Social-Democratic workers and functionaries that the Communists are even disposed to make concessions in the interests of establishing the united front of Communist and Social-Democratic workers against the bourgeoisie. We wish to declare openly and unreservedly: The renunciation of polemics against the Social-Democratic Parties, during the period of common struggles against the offensive of capital, against fascism and imperialist war, is a concession.

Concession to Strengthen Fight

We are making this concession despite the fact that we are firmly convinced that our polemics against the supporters of class collaboration with the bourgeoisie are not only well founded but that such polemics constitute an indispensable part of workers' democracy. This workers' democracy consists not least in the fact that the workers — members of one and the same class but holding different views — convince one another in the struggle of ideas. Workers' democracy denotes not only the right, but also the duty of mutual conviction. In return for this concession on our part, we ask nothing of the Social-Democratic Parties, but the enlisting of all workers in the common front of struggle against the common class enemy.

We Communists will never, under any circumstances, repudiate our principles, our tactics. We will never give our consent to the collaboration of the working class with its class enemy, the bourgeoisie. We were, are and always will be for the revolutionary overthrow of bourgeois rule in all its forms — whether fascist or bourgeois-democratic. We are for the unrestricted power of the working class, for the dictatorship of the proletariat, for Soviet power, which can only be set up by the use of proletarian force against bourgeois force — by revolution. We have proved by the example of the Soviet Union that only the dictatorship of the proletariat, only Soviet power can bring about the broadest democracy of all toilers and clear the way for Socialism. But to those workers who do not yet share our views on all these question of principle, we have always addressed the call: Struggle with us against the common class enemy, against the most immediate dangers which are threatening the proletariat. On January 1, 1922, when the offensive of capital against the international working class set in, we addressed ourselves to proletarian men and women in all countries with the following words:

146

"You do not yet dare to struggle in the new way, you do not yet dare to struggle for power, for dictatorship, with arms in your hands. You do not yet dare to make the great attack on the citadels of world reaction. At least, then, rally together for the struggle for bare life, for the struggle for peace. Rally for this struggle in a fighting front. Rally together as a proletarian class against the bourgeois class. Tear down the barriers which have been set up between you. Take your places in the ranks, whether Communist, Social-Democrat, Anarchist, or Syndicalist, for the struggle against the emergency of the hour. The Communist International has always called upon the workers who stand for the dictatorship of the proletarians, for the Soviets, to unite in independent parties. It does not take back one word of what it has said in arguing for the formation of independent Communist Parties; it is convinced that every passing day will convince ever greater masses how right it has been in all its conduct and actions. But despite everything which divides us, it says: Proletarian men and women, close up the ranks for the struggle for that which you all feel to be the common goal."

* * *

Once again the Communists say to the workers of Social-Democratic and reformist organizations and to their functionaries: Do you not feel that the advance of fascism in a number of countries, the direct preparations which are being made for a new imperialist slaughter of the peoples, the further degradation of the position of the working class, must unite us? You follow your leaders, who, as we are convinced, pursue an incorrect policy, the policy of class collaboration, a policy which does not correspond to the interests of the proletariat but to those of the bourgeoisie. We believe that our criticism of your Party is correct. But the attacks on the policy of your leaders were not, for us, an end in themselves; they were always and

147

they still are a means in the struggle for establishing the unity of the working class against capitalism.

In order to break the bonds of class collaboration with the bourgeoisie — bonds which hold fast such an important part of the working class as the adherents of Social-Democracy represent — in order that we may be able jointly to wage a common struggle against the common enemy, in order to achieve this minimum which is necessary for successful struggle against fascism, we were, are, and remain ready to make this concession to your leaders. We steadfastly hope that the common struggle of Communist and Social-Democratic workers — even though it means temporarily abandoning an important condition of workers' democracy, polemics against incorrect policy — that this struggle will convince the Social-Democratic workers that the sole correct tactic of the working class is not the reformist policy, not class collaboration with the class enemy, but the irreconcilable revolutionary class struggle against capitalism and its rule.

C. P. Will Follow Stern Path

It follows from this conviction that the Communist Parties will not let themselves be deterred, either by the courteous or by the malicious refusals of any Social-Democratic Party, from pursuing the path of consistent struggle for the unity of action of the proletariat.

No matter what answers are given by the Social-Democratic leaders to our proposals for unity of action, we will call upon the proletarians, no matter to what party they may belong, to engage in common action against capitalism, fascism and imperialist war, for the defense of the living interests, for the defense of the rights of the workers. We are ready to make proposals to the leaders of the Social-Democratic Parties as well; we are ready to negotiate. But we know that it is our absolute duty to make these proposals not only to the Social-Democratic Party leaders, that it is our duty not to conduct our negotiations behind the scenes. If some Communists have not learned this, they must now above all realize that every proposal made to a Social-Democratic Party executive or to the leaders of a reformist trade union, must be backed up by hundreds of applications to all organizations of the Social-Democratic Parties and reformist trade unions.

Broad Mass Work Necessary

By means of broad mass work we must ensure that the adherents of the Social-Democratic Parties, the members of reformist trade unions, know of every proposal made by a Communist Party for joint action against the class enemy. If the Communists in France, in Switzerland or in England, have neglected to make proposals of action every day in the Social-Democratic Party organizations through delegations and in the local organizations of the reformist trade unions through the Communist groups, if they have neglected to hold joint meetings of Communist and Social-Democratic workers, this was unquestionably a mistake. Such a militant campaign for unity of action as is represented by the proposals for the rescue of Thaelmann, for the struggle against German fascism, must be spread abroad in tens and hundreds of thousands of leaflets, must be accompanied by the resolutions of hundreds of Communist and Social-Democratic organizations, staffs of factories, etc.

Only such a broad common struggle of Communist and Social-Democratic trade union members, of members of reformist and of revolutionary organizations, while drawing in the broadest sections of the unorganized proletarians, can bring about unity of action. What has been let slip hitherto in this campaign against fascism and for the rescue of Thaelmann, must be made good in the immediate future.

Communists Do Not Stop Halfway

We shall not tire of the struggle for unity of action! We

shall achieve it despite all, in spite of everything! Again and yet again we say to the Social-Democratic workers: You do not know us Communists if you think that we are going to stop half way. The struggle for the united front of the working class is a point in the program of the Communist International, and we, whose actions never belie our words, take our program seriously. Despite diplomacy, despite rude refusals or silence in answer to our proposals, we shall turn to you again, ready to struggle together with you against capitalism, against imperialist war, against fascism, for our common class interests and against the emergency of the day.

You Social-Democratic workers should not stop half way either. Join the ranks in the united action of the working class for victory over the class enemy.

Any Argument Is Good Enough

As the events in the struggle for unity of action have shown, it is becoming increasingly less possible simply to pass over in silence the offers made by the Communist Parties to the Social-Democratic Parties and their organizations. The working class's urge to unity on the one hand, and on the other hand the pressure brought to bear by the bourgeois allies, are compelling the Social-Democratic Party leaders to give open answers to the offers made. And just because of this urge to unity on the part of the working class, they are compelled to produce argument for the rejection of these offers.

It must be said that these arguments do not look as if their inventors had wasted much pains upon them. It denotes, to some extent, an under-estimation of the mental requirements and political level of the Social-Democratic workers when the Social-Democratic leaders deem that they can convince their followers with arguments such as these. True, it must be granted that it is an extremely difficult task to find even the semblance of an argument for rejecting the idea of unity of action. Nevertheless, it would seem that the Social-Democratic Party leaders, who reject the offers of the Communist Parties, take very little trouble to produce their arguments in such a way that the members of their parties may at any rate receive the impression that their leaders are seriously considering the possibilities of setting up a broad united front against fascism and the offensive of capital.

None the less, we feel ourselves obliged to answer these arguments. Let us take the most typical of the reasons put forward as grounds for rejecting the Communist Parties' proposals to organize the joint struggle against the common class enemy; and let us answer these arguments seriously, devoting to the task that seriousness with which not only Communists but also Social-Democratic workers are fighting for unity of action.

"We Are Insulted"

Most of the Social-Democratic Party leaders reject the proposals for a united front on the grounds that they feel themselves to have been insulted by the Communists. We find this most clearly expressed in the answer given by the Party executive of the German Social-Democratic Labor Party in Czechoslovakia. In this letter (published in the Prague Sozialdemokrat of July 18, 1934) we read as follows:

"We are astounded that, after all you have done in long years of work to prevent common actions of the whole proletariat, you should approach us with an offer like this. We do not understand how, after you have for years hurled the epithet of 'social-fascist' at us, you can call upon us for common struggle against fascism. We cannot grasp how you can invite us to joint combatting of the war danger when you have slandered us as 'instigators of war' and 'social-imperialists.' . . . We are thus unable to organize any joint actions with you, since it is impossible for us to join you in your policy of insincerity and double dealing and since the most elementary claims of self-respect forbid us to allow

151

ourselves to be simultaneously wooed and spat upon by you."

If I were a Social-Democratic worker, I would have told my leaders the following in this connection:

Questions to Social-Democratic Leaders

"You sit in one government together with a number of bourgeois politicians who in the past have ruthlessly persecuted the Social-Democratic workers. This has been the case in every country where Social-Democratic Party leaders sat or sit together in one government with bourgeois politicians. The fact that the bourgeois parties, in conjunction with which the Social-Democratic Party leaders look after the business of the bourgeois state, have also persecuted Social-Democratic workers, did not prevent you from forming a coalition with them. When, for example, Vandervelde, the chairman of the Second International, entered the government, he most probably took his seat beside bourgeois ministers who in his youth had heaped abuse upon him as a Social-Democrat, or even persecuted him.

"When at the beginning of the imperialist war it was proclaimed that the nation was in danger, did you not "bury the hatchet" with the leaders of bourgeois parties, did you not join hands with them? Now, however, it is a real danger which is threatening our class — the danger of fascism, the danger of the offensive of capital. How can I, a simple member of my party, understand how it was that the proclamation of danger to the country caused my leaders to become reconciled with the class enemy, whereas now the real danger menacing our class cannot induce these same leaders to enter into common action with my class comrades from the Communist Party for the interests of my class against the dangers with which the class enemy is threatening us?

What Are the Real Obstacles?

"It is true that the Communists have called the Social-Democratic leaders social-fascists and social-imperialists. I did not agree with this, despite the fact that the Communists never treated me as a social-fascist or a social-imperialist, since I was their work-mate and a rank-and-file member of my party. I am glad that it has come to this — that the Communist Parties have declared in the interests of the unity of action of the whole working class that they will cease making attacks on the Social-Democratic leaders during the period of joint actions. It is all the more incomprehensible to me that my party leaders should want to treat the hard words that have been said as a permanent obstacle to the united action of the working class, whereas the Communist Parties, whose leaders and members have been not only abused but also fired upon by many Social-Democratic leaders, stretch out their hand to us for struggle against the common class enemy.

"I cannot understand why the Social-Democratic leaders want to take hard words as a permanent obstacle to unity of action at a time when, for example, the Communist Party of Czechoslovakia, whose leaders Gottwald and Kopetzki were persecuted by the Social-Democratic Minister of Justice, nevertheless, in spite of everything, offers unity of action together with the Social-Democratic Party against the bourgeoisie. If the dead bodies of Rosa Luxemburg and Karl Liebknecht and so many tens of thousands of proletarians who were the victims of Noske and similar Social-Democratic leaders, do not keep the Communists from joint action together with us, when it is a question of warding off the fascist danger, of the struggle against fascism, why then should the hard words once spoken against our leaders keep us from common struggle together with the Communists?"

This is the least which I would have answered my leaders had I been a Social-Democratic worker.

"The Second International Does Not Permit..."

In its letter of July 18 (published in Le Peuple) the Central Committee of the Belgian Labor Party rejected the united front proposal of the Communist Party with the following argument:

"It is, however, impossible to contemplate the formation of the united front which you have proposed to us. The Socialist and Labor International has made distinct proposals to the Communist International. We are therefore of the opinion that it is the business of these two authorities, upon which we are dependent, to bring about the agreement which is required."

In answer to this, a Social-Democratic worker should say to his party comrades:

"Have you ever noticed that our party was dependent in its decisions upon the Second International? In all articles by Vandervelde in our party newspaper, I have always read that it is only the Communist Parties which are dependent upon their International in Moscow. I cannot even now understand why it is that our Social-Democratic Party friends in France are able to enter into common struggle with the French Communists against fascism, against the dangers of the day, whereas we in Belgium are not allowed to do so. Hitherto, all we have heard is that we Social-Democrats, in contrast to the Communists, do not let our tactics be dictated to us from outside, but decide them ourselves in accordance with the conditions in our own country. I even read an article in Le Peuple of July 19, translated from the central organ of Dutch Social-Democracy, Het Volk, in which the same idea is expressed:

"We suppose that there is no single Socialist in the world who would not be ready most cordially to welcome the unity of all Socialist Parties. But that is not the point. We must face reality and seek for a means of changing the present situation in which the working class is split, and of

forging the unity of the working class. These means differ in every country."

"The Communist International also said in its appeal that the question of unity of action should be solved in accordance with the peculiarities of the various countries and parties.

"Diplomatic Subterfuge"

"Why then does my party invoke the decision of the Socialist and Labor International, which forbids all sections of the Social-Democratic International to negotiate with the Communist Parties? They should not play diplomatic tricks with us Social-Democratic workers. In France it is permitted, but in Belgium it is forbidden! I could have understood it if our Belgian party leaders had demanded other conditions, other slogans than in France; but I cannot understand why they should reject the offer of the Communists unconditionally. It ought to be openly stated whether our party leaders want unity of action against the bourgeoisie with the Communists, with all workers, or whether they do not. Diplomatic subterfuge, however, should be used by them against the class enemy and not against members of their own party.

"I am heart and soul on the side of proletarian internationalism. I am an enemy of nationalism, for during the imperialist war I have learned, from my own personal experience, that the defense of the nation in a capitalist state is the defense of the interests of the ruling class. But it is a fine sort of 'proletarian internationalism' if it means that unity of action for combatting the international danger of fascism and imperialist war is internationally forbidden."

"The United Front Is a Soviet Maneuver."

"The United Front Is in Contradiction to the Foreign Policy of the Soviet Union."

Both of these arguments are everywhere current where people are trying to disseminate mistrust in unity of action or to fight against it.

Reporting Leon Blum's speech at the National conference of the Socialist Party of France, the Populaire of July 16, 1934, writes as follows:

"Leon Blum does not believe that the change in the attitude of the Communist Party is inspired by its internal position, nor by the internal policy of the Russian section of the Third International, but rather by the foreign policy of the Soviet Union."

The Paris correspondent of the Swiss Social-Democratic paper Volksrecht sent the following report regarding the struggle for unity of action in France (July 19, 1934):

"The Soviet Union, which is staking everything to incorporate itself in the commonwealth of nations and which, on account of its international relations, would thus have us forget the formerly so strongly emphasized antagonism both against Western capitalism and also against Western democracy, is interested in adapting the Communist Parties to these tendencies."

In direct contradiction to these assertions, the leaders of German Social-Democracy in Czechoslovakia produce the following arguments:

"You reproach us with the fact that we agree to the military budget. Quite apart from the fact that the Communist Party in the Soviet Union gives its consent to the expenditure of billions for armaments purposes, this reproach is altogether grotesque in the present situation and

156

stands in complete contradiction to the foreign policy of the Soviet Union, support for which you demand from us."

What, then, is the Social-Democratic worker to think? Is the struggle of the Communist Parties for unity of action against the bourgeoisie a Soviet plot or a counter-revolutionary subterfuge, perhaps even a maneuver of white guard Russian emigrants? And if he is to be clear about it all, he must first ask: What proposals have the Communist Parties made to the Social-Democratic Parties?

The Communist Answer

The answer is clear: A united front, common action by both parties and their supporters against their own bourgeoisie, against fascism in Germany and in their own countries, against the danger of fascization, against the offensive of capital on the working class in all its forms.

He should also reflect on the question: Have the Communists anywhere or at any time opposed the actions of the working class against the bourgeoisie or the unity of these actions?

The answer can only be: No, the Communists were never opposed to such actions, never opposed to the unity of action of the whole proletariat against the bourgeoisie.

Another question which the Social-Democratic worker must ask himself is as follows:

Is the Soviet Union, under all circumstances, interested that the proletarians in capitalist countries should fight united against their bourgeoisie, or does the attitude of the Soviet Union toward the united front of the workers in bourgeois states depend on the "foreign political situation of the moment"?

Cites Stalin's Writings

He can find the answer to this question in the works of

the most acknowledged leader of Bolshevism. Stalin writes as follows in his work Foundations of Leninism on the relation between the Soviet State and the proletariat of capitalist countries.

"The THIRD STAGE [i.e., the third stage of the Russian Revolution — B. K.] commenced after the October Revolution. Aim: Consolidation of the dictatorship of the proletariat in one country, USING IT AS THE STRONGHOLD FOR THE OVERTHROW OF IMPERIALISM IN ALL COUNTRIES. The revolution goes beyond the confines of one country and the period of world revolution commences. The main forces of the revolution: THE DICTATORSHIP OF THE PROLETARIAT IN ONE COUNTRY AND THE REVOLUTIONARY MOVEMENT OF THE PROLETARIAT IN ALL COUNTRIES." (My emphasis — B. K.)

A plain answer to a plain question! It can never be to the interest of the Soviet Union that the proletariat in capitalist countries should pursue the policy of class collaboration with its own bourgeoisie.

Nevertheless, the Social-Democratic worker can retort: That is all very fine! I don't doubt that Stalin is the greatest revolutionary of the present day. But that doesn't alter the fact that the Soviet Union concludes treaties with bourgeois governments, whereas the Communist Parties call upon us to struggle against these governments. There is something wrong here!

U.S.S.R. Is International Bulwark

We Communists answer as follows: It may perhaps sound perplexing to some, since it is here a question of struggles in which world historical questions are being decided. But there is nothing wrong here — in fact, quite the contrary.

The Soviet Union, for the time being the sole proletarian

state which, as experience shows, is the bulwark of the whole international proletarian revolution, nay, of the bourgeois-democratic national liberation struggles of all oppressed peoples, is indeed obliged to conclude treaties with the governments of capitalist states. It even makes efforts to secure such treaties in order to guarantee peace for itself and for the whole of mankind. The Soviet Union is compelled to do this in just the same way as the workers in capitalist countries are compelled, so long as they have not taken possession of the capitalist enterprises by way of revolution, to conclude agreements with the capitalist employers. We Communists hold that the workers, if they were not split but were united on the basis of our program, would long ago have been able to overthrow capitalism, just as the Russian proletarians did under the leadership of the Bolsheviks. But until capitalism has been overthrown, we Communists hold that the workers — no matter to what party or organization they may belong — should fight for collective agreements, for better wage agreements with the employers. So long as the relation of forces between bourgeoisie and proletariat is such that the capitalists remain masters of the means of production, we will always fight to see to it that the workers in their hard struggle against the employers may force the latter through collective agreements to give them better conditions of work.

Favor Collective Agreements

The Soviet Union does likewise. The capitalists still rule on five-sixths of the earth's surface. The Soviet Union must conclude the treaties with the states of these capitalists until the workers have overthrown the rule of their bourgeoisie.

We Communists are in favor of collective agreements in the interests of the workers. But we are deadly enemies of the reformist policy of class collaboration, which is based on the theory of the so-called community of interests of workers and employers. We will never agree to such class collaboration with

159

the bourgeoisie. This, however, cannot prevent us from recommending the workers to take advantage of the contradiction among the individual capitalist employers. If the workers in one branch of industry are on strike, or are locked out by the employers, and some of the employers are compelled, for one reason or another, to grant the demands of their workers, to put an end to the lockout, no reasonable strike leader will say: The workers ought to scorn the concessions of these employers and not try to take advantage of the difficulties of the individual capitalists, of the contradictions of the capitalists among themselves, for the benefit of those who are on strike or locked out.

* * *

The Soviet Union pursues the same proletarian policy in the domain of its foreign political relations: it takes advantage of the contradictions between the capitalist states in its foreign policy. It does this in the interests both of the toilers of the Soviet Union and of the whole world proletariat. It does this, for example, when, after the exit from the League of Nations of the two most bellicose imperialist states, Japan and Germany, it contemplates entering the League of Nations itself.

But the Soviet Union does not therefore pursue a "League of Nations" policy, any more than revolutionary workers, when they conclude a collective agreement, are pursuing a policy of class collaboration. The Soviet Union, when it enters the League of Nations, will pursue a Soviet policy, just as revolutionary workers, in an enterprise where they are working on the basis of a collective agreement, pursue a policy of class struggle.

Defense of Socialist Construction

However, the Social-Democratic worker may ask

further:

Very well! But why do the Communists demand that we should be against agreeing to the war budget when the Communist Party in the Soviet Union — as the German Social-Democrats in Czecho-Slovakia say in their answer — "gives its consent to the expenditure of billions for armaments purposes"? Why should not our members of Parliament do the same?

No, we answer. The Communist Party of the Soviet Union does not give its consent to the spending of billions for armaments purposes, it decides upon this expenditure for the defense of its socialist construction, which is continually threatened, in accordance with the foreign political situation, now by this group of imperialist states, now by that. It decides upon this expenditure by order of the proletariat, for the defense of the proletariat against those armies, the money for whose arming is voted by the Social-Democratic members of Parliament.

Socialist Party Aids Arms Expenditures

On the other hand a Social-Democratic Party — even in the most democratic capitalist states — gives its consent when it agrees to the armaments expenditure which has been decided upon by the bankers, factory owners and big agrarians.

The difference, therefore, is obvious, just as crystal clear as the perpetual and indivisible community of interests, independent of all foreign political circumstances, between the Soviet proletariat and the working class in capitalist countries and their unity in action against the bourgeoisie of all countries.

Anyone who foolishly talks about the united front policy of the Communist Parties being dependent upon the "changing foreign political situation of the Soviet Union" should bear in mind two historical facts:

Cites Mistake in Hungary

1. In 1919 we Hungarian Communists made the great historical mistake that we united our Party with the whole Social-Democratic Party and thus made our policy dependent upon the reformists. The foreign political situation of the Soviet Union was at that time the most difficult imaginable. It was fighting against military intervention, against internal counter-revolution supported by eighteen states. Nevertheless, this foreign political situation did not prevent the leaders of the Soviet Union from warning the Communists in Hungary of the dangers involved in this incorrect policy of the united front.

2. Again, when it became clear that the Anglo-Russian Committee, the joint committee of the English and Soviet trade unions, in consequence of the treachery of the "Left" English trade union leaders, was not serving the interests of the English and of the international proletariat, but was injuring these interests, the Communist Party of the Soviet Union did not hesitate an instant in recommending the dissolution of this committee, which had for a certain time been necessary in the interests of the proletariat.

Let the Social-Democratic workers decide for themselves whether the Communist Parties, which have made the united front, the struggle for the unity of action of the working class, a part of their program, are pursuing a policy based on principle or one which can be described as a policy of opportunism.

The Legend of the "Non-Aggression Pact"

The Populaire of June 23 published an article by Leon Blum entitled "Unity of Action" — an article in which he expressed himself against unity of action. The editorial board of the Populaire, of which Leon Blum is political head, supplemented this article by a trick. On the pretext that the editors of the paper, "in view of the armistice of the bourgeois parties," desire "the armistice of the proletarian parties," it

162

published two documents side by side: the text of the Franco-Soviet Non-Aggression Pact and the draft of a "Socialist-Communist Non-Aggression Pact."

If I were a member of the French Socialist Party, I would have answered this article of Leon Blum and the trick of his editorial board as follows:

"Dear Leon Blum and dear editors of the Populaire: "I am in favor of the unity of action of all French proletarians, whether Socialists, Communists, Confederatives or Unitarian trade unionists. I am in favor of it with my whole heart and with my whole understanding. I demand of the leaders of the Communist Party of France, as well as of the leaders of my own party, that they take this unity of action, and also us individual workers, seriously. But I protest against the fact that you, dear Leon Blum and the editors of the Populaire, are so little disposed to take us seriously that in the central organ of the French Socialist Party — surely not with the intention of forging a document — you have reprinted the Non-Aggression Pact between France and the Soviet Union in a falsified form. Among the names which are here produced as signatories to the pact, the name of the Soviet Ambassador in Paris, Dovgalevsky, is preceded by that of Comrade Stalin, general secretary of the Communist Party of the Soviet Union. We Socialist workers, too, know that Comrade Stalin is a statesman of world historical importance, but we know equally well that he is not a state functionary of the Soviet Union and therefore does not sign any international treaties.

Attacks Blum's Frivolity

"We would prefer it if the editors of the Populaire, upon such a serious occasion, did not display such frivolity.

"But still more strongly do I protest against the fact that the editors of the Populaire regard our relation to our Communist class comrades as identical with the relation between the Socialist Soviet Union and the bourgeois Republic

163

of France. Do you not think that this is an insult to the Socialist workers?

"Despite the vast number of articles by O. Rosenfeld published in the Populaire, we know that the Soviet Union is a proletarian state. Despite the articles of Frossard, we know that France is a republic of French imperialism. We also know that the Soviet Union, as a proletarian state, has made the cause of peace its own cause. It is interested in doing so since peace is necessary for the continuation and completion of the work of socialist construction. To me it is quite clear that the Soviet Union concludes treaties with all bourgeois states in order to secure peace. This also serves the interests of the whole international proletariat. We know likewise that the Soviet Union cannot overthrow the capitalist world by itself, and it is therefore compelled, in order to prolong the period of respite which has set in after the termination of military intervention, to come to agreements with imperialist states as well. It will be compelled to do so until the contracting parties, for example in France, are no longer Herriot or Dournergue, but representatives of the French working class. The Soviet Union and the capitalist world exist side by side, but they are also opposed to one another. They represent two hostile classes, two mutually opposed systems — the working class and the bourgeoisie, the system of socialism and the system of capitalism.

"Can you wonder, dear Leon Blum and the editors of the Populaire, if I feel insulted at the fact that you pretend that my relation to my workmates who are organized in the Communist Party is the same as the relation between the Socialist Soviet Union and imperialist France? Can my relation and the relation of my party to the Communist Party of France and to its members, be considered as similar to the relations between Lebrun, Herriot and Barthou on the one hand, and Stalin, Litvinov and Dovgalevsky on the other? Are we, my comrade at the work-bench and I, two different representatives of two hostile classes like Stalin and Lebrun, Litvinoff and Herriot, Dovgalevsky and Barthou?

"I have placed great faith in you. But how can you expect me to believe you when you try to represent me, a class conscious French worker, as an equally great enemy of my Communist workmate as the system of capitalism is to the system of socialism?

"No! I do not agree to this! An armistice, a non-aggression pact is not enough for me. Such methods are right when applied to the relations between the proletarian Soviet Union and bourgeois France. But it is a form of sabotage of unity of action when this system of non-aggression pacts is applied to the relations between Socialist and Communist workers — members of one and the same class. It is not an armistice or a nonaggression pact which the must conclude with the Communist Party. The growth of the fascist danger in France, the increase of preparation for war throughout the whole world, demands something quite different. What existed between us Socialist workers and the Communist workers between February 6 and 12 this year, was not an armistice, not a diplomatic treaty, not a nonaggression pact. During these days we Socialist and Communist workers stood shoulder to shoulder in armed alliance against the attack of fascism. With brilliant success we repulsed the impudent attack of fascism (supported by M. Chiappe), and proceeded to take the offensive. We workers are proud to have stood shoulder to shoulder with our Communist brothers in united action against the bourgeoisie. So let us leave diplomacy to the diplomats. Let us avoid giving even the outward impression that the relation between members of the Socialist and Communist Party is that of two opposed classes. Throw aside diplomatic tricks and let us honestly grasp the fraternal hand of the Communist Party in order to defend ourselves in common against the common enemy."

"The United Front With the Communists Repels the Petty Bourgeoisie from the Proletariat"

The Populaire of July 17, 1934, published the draft

resolution which Frossard and his intimate comrades of the Right Wing of French Social-Democracy put forward in the National Council of the French Socialist Party against the acceptance of the Communist offer. In this draft we read as follows:

"... **Merely in order to co-operate with them [i.e., the Communists — B.K.], the Socialist organizations cannot surrender their contact with all the democratic elements, which constitute the enormous majority of the French population.**"

Citizen Frossard cannot be accused of inconsistency. During his brief stay in the Right Wing of the Communist Party of France, he was just as much opposed to the united front with the Social-Democratic Party as now, when he occupies a place in the Right Wing of French Social-Democracy, fulfilling the function of connecting link with the Neo-Socialists and fulminating against the united front with the Communist Party. It was this same Frossard who, while still in the ranks of the Communist Party of France, wrote as follows against the leadership of the Communist International, against its directives for the struggle for the united front:

"**For the international Communist front the following holds true: The bridges have been broken; we shall not restore them, nay, not even by coming to terms shall we make this appear desirable in the eyes of the masses.**"

Now, too, Frossard wants to break down the bridges between Social-Democratic and Communist workers, though it is now from the other bank that he is trying to do this. We do not want to force our organizational principles upon the Social-Democratic Parties, but we cannot avoid mentioning that we Communists did not tolerate in our ranks such an attitude to the united front, to the fighting unity of the working class.

Now, however, let us come to the point, to the question

166

whether the unity of action of the working class, the fighting unity of the Social-Democratic workers with the Communist workers is repelling all democratic elements from the working class. Under the term "democratic elements" we are to understand the urban petty bourgeoisie, poor and middle peasants, office employes and professional men.

The Social-Democratic worker, or even the Social-Democratic functionary, whose mental horizon is not limited by the frontiers of his own country, would do well to begin by comparing the successes of the Social-Democratic and of the Communist policy in the ranks of these democratic elements on the basis of concrete examples — Russia on the one hand and on the other hand, Germany and Austria.

The revolutionary policy of the Russian proletariat under the leadership of the Bolshevik Party has made it possible for the Russian working class, numerically a very small proletariat, to lead dozens of millions of poor and middle peasants, broad strata of the office employes and a part of the intelligentsia into the struggle against the big bourgeoisie, the feudal nobility, into the struggle for the power of the proletariat. Today, thanks to the Bolshevik policy, the great majority of the poor and middle peasants in the Soviet Union are collective farmers, conscious builders of the socialist economy. The urban petty bourgeoisie in the Soviet Union are freed from the exploitation of the banks and cartels, united in industrial co-operatives by means of assistance, financial and otherwise, from the state. With tremendous exertions the Bolsheviks have succeeded in saving large sections of the old intelligentsia for socialism. It would be absurd to assert today, as was alleged by many Social-Democrats formerly, that a working class comparatively small in number and the still smaller Bolshevik Party are capable of directing a state and of building up a new socialist economy by means of terror, against the will of the great majority of the population. On the contrary, it has only been possible to carry out this task because the Communist Party has known how to pursue a correct policy in relation to the middle classes. It has been able to do so precisely because the majority of the working class, nay the whole proletariat, has been and is behind it. Only because of this has it been able to throw into the scale the strength of the whole working class in order to lead the middle strata in town and country and to make concessions to the peasantry when the economic situation, the relation of forces between classes, rendered this necessary.

Why has not the relation of the middle strata in town and country toward the working class been the same in Germany and Austria as in Russia? Why did not the broad strata of the urban petty bourgeoisie, of the poor and middle peasantry, take the side of the proletariat when the question of the struggle between labor and capital was raised? Why did they take the side of the fascists, of finance capital, of the great landowners?

The Social-Democratic Parties in Germany and Austria have alleged that the tactics of the Communists repel the petty bourgeois strata in town and country from the working class. We Communists have already said: The petty bourgeois policy of the Social-Democratic Parties renders it impossible to draw over the urban and rural middle strata to the side of the proletariat.

And we repeat now that precisely the petty bourgeois policy of the Social-Democratic Parties was mainly responsible for the fact that these strata have been repelled from the working class, in contrast to Russia, where the proletarian policy of the Bolsheviks against capital, against the big landowners, has drawn these strata into the struggle against capitalism.

What is the peculiarity of the petty-bourgeois policy? Shortly expressed, it is: vacillation between labor and capital, vacillation between the struggle for the interests of the toilers against capital and the defense of capitalist private property against the proletariat! From this vacillation it follows that the petty-bourgeoisie would like to avoid the class struggle and wants to reconcile the interests of labor and capital. Such reconciliation, however, is impossible. This is shown not least by the so-called abolition of the class struggle by the National-Socialists in Germany, which has led only to a tremendous accentuation of class contradictions.

By striving to attain a reconciliation between capital and labor, the petty-bourgeois policy serves the capitalist class, which is interested in seeing that the workers do not wage a class struggle. It is just this which constitutes the reactionary element in the petty-bourgeois policy.

What was the result of the petty-bourgeois policy of Social-Democracy in Germany?

What Happened in Germany?

It did not deal a death blow at monopoly capital, the banks, the factory owners, the Junkers; it showed that it desired peaceful collaboration between all classes and all social strata of the Weimar Republic. It therefore placed itself on the side of the bourgeoisie against the working class. This alone provided a basis for the policy of Noske, Ebert, Zoergiebel and Wels. Social-Democracy participated in the bourgeois governments; it "tolerated" the bourgeois government. Whom did the Social-Democratic Party of Germany tolerate? The governments which looked after the business of big capital and the Junkers and which also exploited the petty bourgeoisie and small peasants. This petty-bourgeois policy of Social-Democracy with the big capitalists and big agrarians thus denotes a collaboration not only with the class enemy of the proletariat, but also with the enemies of the urban petty bourgeoisie and the peasantry.

It is true that the Communists have said hard things about the Social-Democratic Party; they have said that it pursues a petty-bourgeois policy which is directed against the working class but also against the middle classes. The Communist Party has put forward and steadfastly upheld a proletarian policy against the common enemies of the working class and of the middle strata, against the trust magnates, against the big agrarians. It wanted united action on the part of all workers and all middle-class elements against capitalism. The German working class was not split on the question of whether it should join hands with the middle-class elements against capitalism, but on the question of whether it should collaborate with the big bourgeoisie in the interests of big capital, the enemy of the workers and of the middle classes. This collaboration of Social-Democracy with capital has not only split the working class, but has also driven the middle class to the side of capital.

Cites Events in Austria

The effects of a petty-bourgeois policy on the relation between the proletariat and the middle classes in town and country may be seen still more clearly in the case of Austria.

Austrian Social-Democracy veiled its policy with revolutionary phrases. It declared that its main reason for rejecting the Bolshevik policy was that this policy repelled the petty-bourgeois masses from the workers. It even proclaimed that it would realize Socialism through its policy in Vienna. It boasted of the fact that by means of the taxation policy of the well-known Viennese City Councillor, Breitner, the costs of "socialist construction" would be covered without the expropriation of the capitalist enterprises. What actually took place? It was unable with its "democratic socialism" to destroy the sources of capitalist exploitation, of the unearned income of the capitalists. The famous progressive taxation, by means of which Breitner tried to cover the costs of the Viennese municipal policy, did not touch one hair on the head of the Rothschilds; whereas the banking house of Rothschild, with the aid of Social-Democracy, was subsidized at the expense of the small taxpayer. This was also the reason why the small man — the innkeeper, the small shopkeeper, the small tradesman, the small pension-holder, the small and middle peasant — went over into the camp of the National-Socialists, or, into that of the

Heimwehr, of the "Patriotic Front." The Austrian Social-Democrats were also prone to regard the municipal enterprises of Vienna as "a piece of Socialism." But the great municipal enterprise did not compete with the great capitalists; the latter have even pocketed a fair portion of the profits of these concerns through their banks and through their business connections with the Arbeiterbank. "Democratic Socialism" was unable and unwilling to touch capitalist private property, and this petty-bourgeois policy was incapable of winning over the petty-bourgeoisie to the side of the working class.

Agrarian Policy Petty-Bourgeois

The agrarian policy of Austrian Social-Democracy was likewise a petty-bourgeois policy, since it protected the interests of the rich peasants, who formed a community of interests with the big landowners which was bound in practice to work out against the agricultural laborers, the poor and middle peasants. In order "not to repel" the rich peasants (the village bourgeoisie) the Austrian Social-Democrats, when they were in power, did not expropriate the big landowners for the benefit of the poor and middle peasants. They pursued a taxation and credit policy in the court ryside which likewise spared the rich peasants and big landowners.

This petty-bourgeois policy, which left big capital and big landownership untouched, did not give the urban and rural middle classes what both wanted to attain. It could not give it, for this could only be won at the expense of big capital, of the big landlords, of the urban and rural bourgeoisie. This policy has driven large sections of the middle classes in Austria into the camp of fascism.

Class Collaboration With Enemies

On top of all this in both countries came the splitting of the working class in consequence of the class collaboration of Social-Democracy with the enemies not only of the proletariat,

171

but also of the middle classes. A split working class could not summon sufficient strength to make it clear to the middle classes that the latter, in alliance with the working class, could assert their interests against big capital, against the big agrarians. This was the main reason why it was possible for the big capitalists and big agrarians, through the fascist parties, to make use of the anti-capitalist sentiments of the small tradesmen, small shopkeepers, small pension-holders, poor and middle peasants, office employees, etc., in the interests of capitalist private property and of the bourgeois state.

The example of the joint demonstrations of Social-Democratic and Communist workers since February 6, 1934, in France shows that it is not the fascist organizations, but precisely the working class which gains influence among the middle classes as a result of united action by the two parties.

The proletarian revolutionary policy, resolute revolutionary action against capital by means of a firm united front of the working class paralyzes the vacillations of the middle strata and wins over sections of them for the struggle. The petty-bourgeois policy, on the other hand, the policy of reconciliation with capital drives the middle strata into the camp of fascism.

Every Social-Democratic worker or functionary can decide whether the unity of action of the Social-Democratic Parties with the Communist Parties against big capital, against the big agrarians repels the petty-bourgeois strata or draws them into the struggle.

"The Intentions of the Communists Cannot Be Honest"

The Right Social-Democrats in France, Vandervelde in Belgium and Otto Bauer in Prague, all Social Democratic papers repeat this assertion in the most varied keys.

They try to bolster up this absolutely unfounded statement by two further allegations.

Firstly, that the Communist Party of France expelled Doroit because he supported the united front;

Secondly, that the offers made by the Communist Parties to the Social-Democratic Parties represented "orders from Moscow."

This, then, is why the Social-Democratic worker is to be mistrustful of the idea of unity of action together with his Communist class comrades against the bourgeoisie.

C. P. Seeks No Middle Course

We Communists consider it very important that a relation of mutual trust should be established between us and the Social-Democratic workers, as is necessary among members of one aim and the same class. One proof of the fact that our offers for unity of action with the Social-Democratic workers are straightforward and honestly meant is that we declare in advance to the Social-Democratic Parties that the Communist Parties refuse to surrender so much as a syllable of their fundamental standpoint on any single question. We declare openly that our persistant striving for the unity of action of the working class does not mean for a moment that we are looking for a middle course between Social-Democracy and Communism, between reformism and revolutionary tactics, or that we would be disposed to adopt such a middle course. We hold that unity of action for the immediate interests of the working class against the bourgeoisie, that the common struggle against the immediate dangers with which the capitalists are threatening all the toilers, is possible at once. This common struggle can be begun without delay, without waiting for the Social-Democratic workers to adopt our program and tactics in their entirety.

Nor do we seek to make a secret of the fact that the Communist Parties of the individual countries are centralized and united in one single world party, in the Communist International. This does not, of course, mean that the leadership of the Communist International itself decides all questions confronting the individual Communist Parties. It is obvious, however, that the decisions of the individual Communist Parties are arrived at on the basis of the program, of the Congress decisions and the resolutions of the Plenums of the Executive Committee of the Communist International.

C. I. Guides Individual Parties

One need not be a detective in order to discover that the offers made by the individual Communist Parties to the Social-Democratic Parties, with a view to establishing unity of action have been made on the basis of the decisions of the Communist International.

Any Social-Democratic worker can convince himself by the study of a public document that the Executive Committee of the Communist International on March 5, 1933, immediately after Hitler's advent to power, recommended its sections to address proposals to the Social-Democratic Party leaders in order that the Social-Democratic and Communist workers might together wage the struggle against fascism and against the offensive of capital. Here is the text of this proposal:

"In the face of fascism, which is attacking the working class of Germany and unleashing all the forces of world reaction, the Executive Committee of the Communist International calls upon all Communist Parties to make one more attempt to establish a united front together with the Social-Democratic working masses through the medium of the Social-Democratic parties. The E. C. C. I. is making this attempt in the firm conviction that the united front of the working class for the struggle against the bourgeoisie would repulse the offensive of capital and of fascism and would hasten on to an extreme degree the inevitable end of all capitalist exploitation.

"In view of the peculiar conditions of individual countries and the difference of the concrete tasks of struggle

174

confronting the working class in each one of them, agreements between the Communist Parties and the Social-Democratic Parties for definite actions against the bourgeoisie can be effected most successfully within the bounds of the individual countries. The E. C. C. I. therefore recommends the Communist Parties to put forward proposals to the respective Central Committees of the Social-Democratic Parties affiliated to the Socialist International regarding joint actions against fascism and the offensive of capital."

Thus if "Moscow" means the leadership of the Communist International and not the Soviet government, then indeed the initiative in this matter comes from "Moscow."

Why Was Doriot Expelled

How, then, can we explain the alleged fact that Doriot was expelled from the Communist Party of France because he was in favor of unity of action — though it is worth noting that he poured out his heart before the correspondent of the fascist Matin, instead of lodging his complaints in "Moscow." If it were true that Doriot had been expelled because he was in favor of the united front, the leadership of the Communist International, "gave orders" for the united front proposals, would surely have received him with open arms and trumpets.

So there must really be something wrong here. Something must be wrong for the simple reason that Doriot wanted not the united front with the Social-Democratic Party but something quite different, on account of which it was impossible for him to remain in the Communist Party.

What did Doriot want? He wanted the Communist Party of France to pursue a Social-Democratic policy! How else are we to explain the great sympathies felt for Doriot by the Social-Democratic Party leaders?

175

Doriot Distorted C. P. Plan

What did Doriot do? He distorted the plan of action of the Communist Party of France for the establishment of unity of action; he distorted it in order to use it against the Party; he gave it out as his own plan and on the basis of this plan tried to incriminate the leadership of the C. P. of France of being against unity of action at a time when Communists and Social-Democratic workers were victoriously defying the attacks of fascism in a united front of struggle on the streets of Paris. He wanted to disintegrate the C. P. of France. How else can we explain the sympathies felt for Doriot by the Trotskyites, who want to disintegrate the Communist Party?

What did Doriot do besides? He violated revolutionary discipline, Party democracy. He acted contrary to the decisions of the great majority of the Party. He set his district against the whole Party. He addressed himself to the bourgeois press, to the Social-Democratic leaders, instead of applying to the Party Conference and there submitting himself and his views to the judgment of the representatives of the whole Party. He tried to split the revolutionary party of the French proletariat. How else can we explain the sympathy felt by the whole bourgeois press, which fears revolution like the plague, for Doriot, who has audaciously followed the path of Briand, Millerand and Viviani — these ex-socialists who looked after the business of the French bourgeoisie as prime ministers of the republic?

How the C. P. Functions

The Communist Party is not a compulsory society; it is based on the voluntary obligation of its members to pursue a revolutionary class policy on the basis of the program of the Communist International and to subject themselves to revolutionary discipline and to the decisions of the majority of the Party.

It has never occurred to us Communists to demand of the Social-Democrats as a condition of unity of action that they

176

should accept our principles and subject themselves to our Party discipline, to the decisions of the majority of our Party. But all the more do we demand this of the members of our Party and all the more yet of such Party members as occupy leading posts in the Communist movement.

The expulsion of Doriot does not show that the Communists are not sincere. It shows, on the contrary that the Communists take seriously what they say and what they write, no matter whether it is a question of the internal affairs of their own Party or of agreements with other Parties.

"Why Just Now?"

We must deal with yet another attempt which is aimed at awakening mistrust among the Social-Democratic workers against unity of action.

The agreement arrived at between the Communist Party of France and the Socialist Party was received by the leaders of the Second International in a way which cannot even be described as "making the best of a bad job"!

The chairman of the Second International, the leader of the Belgian Labor Party, Emile Vandervelde, wrote as follows in his article in Le Peuple, entitled "The International and the Communists" on July 22, 1934:

"The acceptance by our French comrades of the proposal made by the Communist Party for joint action against fascism and war is an event whose range goes far beyond the bounds of the Socialist Party of France. I may say at once that I am in perfect agreement with Leon Blum, Paul Faure and Lebas when I confess that it would have been morally impossible for them to answer this offer with a blank refusal. However, if we bear in mind what was happening only yesterday, the astounding VOLTE-FACE in Communist tactics gives us grounds for justified mistrust."

What interests us here is not Vandervelde's opinion to

the effect that Leon Blum, Paul Faure and Lebas only accepted under "moral pressure" the offer of the Communist Party for common struggle against fascism and imperialist war. This statement of his must be answered by the leaders of the French Socialists. What we want to deal with here is Vandervelde's assertion regarding an "astounding volte-face in Communist tactics" which in his opinion consists in the fact that the Communist Parties have made offers to the leaders of the Social-Democratic Parties with the aim of establishing unity of action.

Nothing Daunts Communists

If Vandervelde is surprised by the patience, by the pertinacity of the Communists in the struggle for unity of action, then he only shows how ill acquainted with the Communists he is. No difficulty, however great, can cause the Communists to give up the struggle for the united front before state power has been won. But if Vandervelde wants to make the Social-Democratic workers believe that it is only in this year that the Communists have made such offers to the Social-Democratic Party leaders, this denotes something more than ignorance; it denotes a definite malicious intention — to sow mistrust among the Social-Democratic workers by hushing up facts which cannot be done away with.

We do not want to go back to the more distant past of ten or twelve years ago, when the Communists proposed common actions against Italian fascism and their proposals were rejected by the Second International. We will take only one or two examples from the more recent past of the international labor movement — examples which show that the Communists have not neglected opportunities of making proposals to the Social-Democratic Parties for common actions against the common class enemy.

Only one or two examples:

Cites Actions in Berlin

In face of the growing advance of the fascist danger, the Berlin district leadership of the Communist Party of Germany addressed itself, in June 1932, to the Berlin district leadership of the Social-Democratic Party of Germany, making proposals for common actions against fascism in Berlin. On the day of the coup d'etat of Von Papen, the German Communists, on July 20, applied to the headquarters of the Social-Democratic Party of Germany and of the German General Confederation of Trade Unions with a view to joint resistance to the fascist terror. When the German bourgeoisie placed power in the hands of Hitler, the Communist Party of Germany, on January 30, 1933, once again applied to the headquarters of the Social-Democratic Party of Germany and of the German General Confederation of Trade Unions with a similar united front proposal aimed at the organizing of a general strike.

All these united front proposals were answered by the Social-Democratic Party and the reformist trade union leaders with a blank refusal. The pretext for rejecting these united front proposals was most clearly expressed by the former Social-Democratic Reichstag President, Loebe, when he declared:

"We Social-Democrats will not undertake anything so long as the government (i.e., the Hitler government — B. K.) remains on a constitutional basis."

Hitler has "constitutionally" thrown the constitution to the four winds. The refusal of the leaders of the Social-Democratic Party of Germany and of the German General Confederation of Trade Unions to use the general strike against Hitler, to establish the unity of action of the German working class against the German bourgeoisie, paralyzed the forces of the German labor movement at the critical historical moment and aided Hitler to get into power.

Socialist Party Leaders Rejected Unity

If Vandervelde has forgotten it, we can remind the Social-Democratic workers of how some Social-Democratic Parties and Party leaders rejected the united front proposals of the Communist Parties which were made on the basis of the appeal of the Communist International of March 5, 1933. The leaders of the British Labor Party answered as follows in reply to the proposal for a united front against Hitler and against the offensive of capital in March, 1933:

"Workers everywhere should strengthen the Labor Party — the spearhead of political power against dictators, fascist or Communist. By solid unity in industrial, economic, and political movements — powerful because they are democratic — British workers can secure their own rights against the ambitious designs of any would-be dictators there may be here at home, and give powerful encouragement to the forces of Democratic Socialism throughout the world." (Daily Herald, March, 1933.)

In order to obtain an idea of how the "forces of democratic socialism" have been strengthened by the policy of the English Labor Party, of how they have fought against Hitler, one should read the organ of German Social-Democracy, Deutsche Freiheit (June 15, 1934), where the following comment is made on the policy of the Labor Party in regard to Germany:

"For some time past it has been a part of the ever more incomprehensible foreign policy of the labor paper (i.e., The Daily Herald — B.K.) to offer its assistance to the fascist governments in Germany and Italy. Mr. Ewer, foreign political editor of this paper, after a short journey through Germany and Italy, has now been singing hymns of praise in honor of Mussolini and pledged himself for Hitler's true love of peace. Even the Storm Troops are described by him as a perfectly harmless and peaceful organization. It would seem that the Labor Party does not

180

yet recognize the great dangers involved in such delusion by its own paper. In foreign politics at the present time it is unfortunately more or less leaderless."

The other Social-Democratic Parties have also rejected the united front proposals of the Communist Parties on the basis of the decision of the leadership of the Second International. This decision says that the Social-Democratic Parties should not conduct any negotiations with the Communist Parties in individual countries.

More than a year of struggle was required before the Social-Democratic Parties in France, in Austria and in the Saar region declared themselves ready for common action with the Communist Parties against fascism.

Can it then be regarded as an "astounding volte-face in Communist tactics" if, after the new lessons which the international working class has received, above all by the defeat of the Austrian workers in February 1934, the Communist Parties have renewed their proposals to the Social-Democratic Parties for a united front against fascism.

Instead of fostering mistrust against unity of action, the Social-Democratic workers would do better to study the question of why the united front was not immediately established, at any rate after Hitler's advent to power. They would do well to examine the reasons why the establishment of the united front against fascism was completely frustrated in 1933 and why the struggle for this united front in 1934 has produced some successes, if only initial ones.

After March 5, 1933, the Communist Parties made the proposal that the Social-Democratic and Communist Parties should fight together against German fascism, against fascism in their own countries, against the offensive of capital.

Instead of aiming at a direct struggle against German fascism and fascism in their own countries, the Social-Democratic Parties aimed at the foreign political isolation of

181

German fascism; they undertook to achieve this isolation of Hitler Germany together with their own bourgeoisie. This was the time when in England no other than Chamberlain delivered a great speech against Hitler Germany. In France there was strong feeling in favor of a preventive war against Germany. In Austria there was an immediate strengthening of the French orientation in foreign politics and Social-Democracy treated Dollfuss as the "lesser evil." In Czecho-Slovakia a struggle was waged against German Nazi fascism in alliance with Czech fascist groups. In Poland there was a strong orientation against Hitler Germany. This was the time when international Social-Democracy conducted a rabid campaign against the Soviet Union because "the Red Army did not march," and placed the proletarian dictatorship in the Soviet Union on a par with the fascist dictatorship in Hitler Germany.

The Second and Amsterdam Internationals declared a boycott against goods from Hitler Germany, without, however, taking any serious steps to put this boycott into effect.

Change of International Situation

Instead of a common struggle of the Social-Democratic Parties together with the Communists against the bourgeoisie in their own countries and against German fascism, the Social-Democratic leaders taught the Social-Democratic workers to put their trust in the isolation of Hitler Germany, which was to be achieved together with the bourgeoisie in their own countries. This was the principal reason why we Communists did not succeed in achieving unity of action with our united front proposals made on the basis of the appeal of the Communist International of March 3, 1933.

Meanwhile, however, there came a change in the international situation — a change which gave direct proof to the Social-Democratic workers of the absolute necessity of unity of action.

This change came about above all at the beginning of

this year. The principal symptoms of this change in the situation have been the following:

1. In England there was a change in the relation of English imperialism towards fascism in Germany. Democratic England for a time became the real protector of Hitter Germany. Fresh signs of disintegration appeared in the system of the French bloc. This was shown in the reorientation of Poland towards Hitler Germany and in vacillations on the part of Belgium in favor of Germany on the question of the arming of German imperialism. The collaboration between Germany and Japan and the danger it represents for peace likewise became clearer to the masses of workers. It has also become clearer for most Social-Democratic workers that, despite the rabid campaign of the Second International, the Soviet Union is the only state which is really defying German fascism. All this has proved to the working masses that the policy of teaching the working class to put its trust in the foreign political isolation of Germany, instead of conducting a struggle against German fascism and fascism in all countries, is bluff, or, at best, an illusion.

Heroism of German C. P.

2. A further factor in bringing about a change in the mood of the workers in favor of the united front has been the heroic. struggle of the Communist Party of Germany against the Hitler dictatorship, as also the heroic struggle of Dimitrov in Leipzig against the fascist regime — a struggle waged on behalf of the Communist International, on behalf of the Communist Party of Germany and on behalf of the whole working class.

3. Moreover, the further advance along the road to fascization made by the bourgeois democratic states in a number of countries and the breakdown of parliamentary methods against this fascization have opened the eyes of many Social-Democratic workers and thus encouraged the struggle for unity of action. We need only give one or two examples: France

— the offensive of fascist organizations and the introduction of the emergency decree system; Czecho-Slovakia — emergency decree regime not only against the German Nazis, but also in the whole sphere of social policy, based on the Czech fascist movements; Belgium — plenary power to act for the government; England — the offensive of the fascist Mosley aided by the newspaper king, Lord Rothermere; Switzerland — the Haeberlin bill against the labor movement and the growing activity of the fascist fronts; advances of the fascists in all Baltic and Balkan countries. In all these countries there has been an increasingly rapid growth of the urge to unity among the workers.

Burial of the Boycott

4. We should also mention the tacit and unhonored burial of the boycott against goods from Hitler Germany. We Communists had predicted that this boycott of goods would not be carried into effect and that the agitation for this boycott would only be carried on so long as the interests of the bourgeoisie in the various countries permitted it. The bankruptcy of the idea of a boycott against goods from Hitler Germany has proved the necessity of a revolutionary struggle against fascism.

5. However, the most important factor causing a change of feeling among the broadest masses of the working class was the collapse of Austrian Social-Democracy in February this year. In Austria it was not only one Social-Democratic Party which collapsed — a party which had boasted of having invented "western methods" of building socialism, involving no sacrifices on the part of the workers. In Austria a clear proof was provided that the unity of a great and powerful Social-Democratic Party does not yet denote the unity of the working class, and that strong militant unity of the working class can only be achieved if the workers in political and trade union organizations reject all class collaboration with the bourgeoisie.

All these phenomena today are to a large extent facts of experience for the Social-Democratic workers and those in reformist organizations, and even for many Social-Democratic and trade union functionaries. The presence of such facts of experience has enabled us to repeat our offers of a united front and has yielded the first successes of these proposals.

Address Unity Proposals

In accordance with our program we have effected a turn in our tactics by so altering the form of our struggle as to address our proposals for unity of action not only to the Social-Democratic workers but also to the leaders of the Social-Democratic Parties.

A Social-Democratic worker, however, may raise the question: "That is all very well, but why did you Communists not make such offers to the Social-Democratic Parties before the fascist danger in Germany was an immediate one?

Why did you not make such proposals before?"

We answer as follows:

Try to imagine what would have been the answer given to our united front proposals by the Prussian Prime Minister Otto Braun, by the German Minister of the Interior Severing, by the Police Presidents Zorgiebel and Grzesinski. All these Social-Democratic leaders have directly served the German bourgeoisie, and the whole apparatus of the Germany Social-Democratic Party was completely merged with the state apparatus of the German bourgeoisie, of German capitalism. To propose a united front at that time to the party leadership of Wels, Severing, Braun, Leipart and the rest, would indeed have been purely a maneuver designed to unmask them; it would have had no other purpose than to show the workers that the Social-Democratic Party, which directly minded the business of the German bourgeoisie, and was directly merged with the state apparatus of this bourgeoisie, did not want to fight together with

185

the Communists against itself. This would not only have been a maneuver; it would have been a stupid maneuver.

The unity of action of the Communist Parties with the Social-Democratic Parties is not possible at any given moment. We Communists do not, under any circumstances, favor a united front only from above, a collaboration of the "party chiefs" behind the backs of the masses. We are always and under all circumstances in favor of common struggle of the Social-Democratic and Communist workers, of the united front from below, and, when this is possible, we favor collaboration with the Social-Democratic Parties on the basis of a concrete program against the bourgeoisie.

Vandervelde knows this very well. He knows the difficulties which arise for the Second International. too, from such a situation, and that is why he could not make the best of the "bad job" which the French Socialists did.

In his article he writes:

"It must at any rate not be kept a secret that before the executive of the Socialist and Labor International things will doubtless not go so smoothly as in the National Council of the Socialist Party of France."

Vandervelde has good grounds for fearing the discussions in the Second International over the question of unity of action.

Cites Austrian Unity Action

It will be very difficult to arrive at a united opinion within the Second International on the unity of action between the Communist Party of Austria and the Austrian revolutionary socialists. The common struggle of the Communists and revolutionary Socialists, which came about against the will of the leaders of the former Social-Democratic Party, is being conducted under the slogan of the revolutionary dictatorship of the proletariat. The Social-Democratic Parties represented in the

186

Second International are such parties as have seats in bourgeois governments, as for example in Sweden and Denmark, or such as are just preparing to take over the ship of state from the bourgeoisie, as for example the British Labor Party. All these Social-Democratic Parties and others as well are opposed in principle to the dictatorship of the proletariat; they make no difference between proletarian dictatorship and the fascist dictatorship of the bourgeoisie.

Will such parties as these be able to tolerate the unity of action of the Social-Democratic Parties with the Communist Parties in France, in the Saar region, and of the revolutionary Socialists with the Communists in Austria? The answer to this will be given in the near future, but we are of the opinion that they will not. They will not tolerate it even if Vandervelde and other leaders of the Second International discover a formula for diplomatic reconciliation. But whatever the Second International may decide, the Communists stand fast by their program; they will carry on the struggle for the unity of action of the proletariat against the bourgeoisie. In these struggles the splitting of the working class will be overcome and the unity of the labor movement achieved!

For the Unity of the Labor Movement

What stood and still stands in the way of establishing the unity of action of the workers? What directly or indirectly has kept many Social-Democratic workers from grasping the honestly offered hand of the Communist Parties in order to fight together shoulder to shoulder with their Communist class comrades against the common enemy?

Leon Blum as Witness

We produce a witness of whom no one can allege that he sympathizes with the Communists. This witness is the most acknowledged leader of French Social-Democracy and of the Second International — Leon Blum. In the Populaire of July 11

187

he made the following admission in regard to this question:

"For years on end, when unity of action was spoken of, we always thought and declared: 'No, not unity of action but organizational unity' ('unite organique'), and we have tried to evade and defer all contact aimed at partial or occasional unity till the day when complete and perfect unity is considered possible. I, myself, was also of this opinion and have spoken in this sense. I have a feeling that today this view is no longer justified and that one cannot extricate oneself from the difficulty by this simple act of evasion."

May we not say that this confession of Leon Blum's is a confession of a system of prolonged sabotage against the unity of action of the working class against the attacks of the class enemy, of the fascist and semi-fascist bourgeoisie? Can we not say that our united front tactics have always been seriously and honestly intended, as the program of the Communist International says, "as a means toward achieving success in the struggle against capital, toward the class mobilization of the masses, and the exposure and isolation of the reformist leaders," who prevent the class mobilization of the masses, the successful struggle against capital and victory over capitalism? Were the proposals of the Communist Party of Germany to the German General Confederation of Trade Unions and the Social-Democratic Party of Germany in July, 1932 and January, 1933, the proposals to call a general strike in order to prevent Hitler's advent to power, Communist maneuvers? Was the proposal of the Communist Party of Austria to the Social-Democratic Party of Austria of March, 1933 for the prevention of the Dollfuss dictatorship, a Communist maneuver? Was the appeal of the Communist International of March 5, 1933, "for the establishment of the united front of struggle with the Social-Democratic working masses through the medium of the Social-Democratic Parties" a Communist maneuver?

Leon Blum informs us how these proposals were

"evaded" when he declares now, after the victory of fascism in Germany and Austria:

"It seems impossible to me today to put forward organizational unity as a method of evading unity of action."

"Today"! The confession comes late, but not too late. There is still time to prevent the victory of fascism in many countries, if one does not "evade" the question of unity of action. The unity of action of the French proletariat on the basis of the offer made by the C. P. of France, which was finally accepted and not evaded by French Social-Democracy, is a sign that the French bourgeoisie will not be able to introduce concentration camps on the fascist model for the French proletariat.

Otto Bauer Against Unity of Action

Otto Bauer, once the leader of the great majority of the Austrian working class, puts the question as follows: Not unity of action, but organizational unity of the labor movement. This means he is aiming at the reunification, after its collapse, of the Social-Democratic Party of Austria. Up to the February days of this year Otto Bauer prevented unity of action by answering every offer of the Communist Party of Austria with the words that the unity of the Austrian labor movement was embodied in the Social-Democratic Party of Austria. Times have changed and the relation of forces between the Communist Party and Social-Democracy has changed too — even Otto Bauer must admit that. But he still continues along the old line; under the pretext of uniting the revolutionary forces he wants the reunification of the bankrupt Social-Democratic Party, that is to say, prolonging the split under the new conditions of fascist dictatorship in Austria.

In an article published in the Arbeiterzeitung, now appearing in Brunn, he writes:

189

"The great majority of the Austrian workers all think alike. Ninety per cent of the workers want irreconcilable revolutionary struggle against fascist dictatorship. Ninety per cent of the workers are convinced that the goal of this revolutionary struggle must be a dictatorship of the proletariat, which shall settle accounts with the murderers of the workers, demolish their apparatus of rule, distribute the estates of the aristocrats, the capitalists and the church among the agricultural laborers, the small tenants and peasants' sons, socialize the big undertakings and enterprises now in possession of big capital, and not until then, when it has fulfilled these historical tasks, set up a commonwealth of freedom and equality for all. Ninety per cent of the workers are agreed in the recognition of the goal and of the way that leads to it. We have unity of thought. This demands also unity of organization. It makes possible the unity of the party."

We agree with those Social-Democratic workers who honestly think that the working class in the various countries is ever more sharply confronted, not only with the question of unity of action but also with the problem of the organizational unity of the labor movement. If one really wants to prevent fascism, to destroy its source — capitalism, if one wants to overthrow the rule of the bourgeoisie, this requires not only a "partial and occasional" unity of action but the organization of all revolutionary workers in one party and the rallying together of the majority of the proletariat, nay, of the majority of the whole toiling people, under the banners of this revolutionary workers' party.

For Overthrow of Capitalism

We Communists hold that the overthrow of capitalism is on the order of the day. In different countries the struggle for the overthrow of capitalism is being conducted on a different level of development, but the objective conditions for this struggle are everywhere maturing.

When we untiringly called upon the workers, no matter to what Party or organization they might belong, when we called upon the Social-Democratic Parties and reformist trade unions to engage in joint actions with us, we always declared:

Form the united front together with us against capital, against its attacks on the toilers, against fascism and the imperialist war which is threatening. Do this no matter what may divide you from us in questions of principle and tactics. We steadfastly adhere to the view that the founding of the Communist Parties and of the Communist International was the first step to unifying the working class on the basis of the class struggle after this basis had been deserted by the Social-Democratic Parties. But we know that the Party is not the whole class; you workers, no matter of what organization, belong to the same class as we, to the class as whose representatives we regard the Communist Parties. The unity of action of the workers against the emergency of the hour, against fascism which is threatening all of us directly or which has already burst upon us, also leads to overcoming the splitting of the labor movement and to establishing organizational unity in it. If you want organizational unity, then first realize unity of action.

Great Single Mass Party

We Communists thus stand for the organizational unity of the labor movement; we stand for a great single mass Party of the proletariat. We think, we hope, that the great majority of the Austrian workers, after the heavy price they have paid for the lessons of the February struggles, really do think alike. We believe that 90 per cent of the Austrian workers already want the irreconcilable revolutionary struggle, also against those who in the hour of the outbreak of the armed struggle sent Christian-Socialist mediators to Dollfuss, the hangmen of the workers, and were willing to recognize the fascist dictatorship for a term of two years. We think that 90 per cent of the workers in Austria are convinced that the goal of a revolutionary struggle is not "a"

191

dictatorship of the proletariat, as Otto Bauer writes, but the dictatorship of the proletariat which the Communist Party of Austria, on the basis of the program of the Communist International, has set the Austrian proletarians as the goal of their struggle. This program, the program of the dictatorship of the proletariat and of the armed struggle for this dictatorship has already — as Otto Bauer must himself acknowledge — organizationally united thousands of former Social-Democratic workers, including leading functionaries, in the most difficult conditions of illegality for revolutionary struggle in the Communist Party of Austria. What, then, stands in the way of uniting the labor movement in Austria? The endeavors of those who are compelled, made wise by the palpable experiences of history, to acknowledge the dictatorship of the proletariat, but who want to prevent a uniting of the Austrian workers on the basis of the program of struggle for the dictatorship of the proletariat which has already been recognized by the Austrian working class, and who even hinder unity of action for more immediate aims.

In various countries there is a different situation in regard to the organizational unity of the labor movement. How far the tactics of one or the other party, of the Communists or Social-Democratic Party, are correct in the common struggle of the working class against the common class enemy — this is being tested by the historical experience of the workers. We Communists have never supposed it possible to overcome the split in the labor movement through organizational union otherwise than by way of the persuading and self-determination of the working masses as to which theory, strategy and tactics are correct — those of the Communists or those of the Social-Democrats.

When unity of action of the Social-Democratic and Communist workers is required for concrete but limited aims of struggle, the Communists say that the working class needs the united front in order to fight against the bourgeois and not in order to collaborate with the bourgeoisie; each remains in his own party but fights in common against the common enemy. But if it is a question of organizational unity, then the Communists say: The working class needs unity in order to conquer the bourgeoisie and not in order to attain a respite, an extra breathing-space for capitalism. In this respect too, the Communists are true to the words of Marx: they do not conceal their aims, they do not manoeuvre in regard to their class comrades. They say quite openly before the Social-Democratic workers that they want to persuade the latter in unity of action, in the common struggle that the correct tactic is not the reformist but the revolutionary tactic; it is not coalition with the bourgeoisie which leads the working class to power, but the armed uprising at the right moment; that there is no such thing as the growing of capitalism into socialism through any spacious plans designed to convince the bourgeoisie that socialism is useful and necessary for the capitalist as well, but that it is only the dictatorship of the proletariat, destroying as it does the forces of the capitalist class, destroying its means of influencing the petty bourgeoisie and small peasant — that it is only this dictatorship of the proletariat which leads to socialism.

Unity of Action and Organizational Unity

The great majority of the working class — we have always known and said this — will be able to choose between the two theories, strategies and tactics only in common struggle. We have set ourselves the task in the program of Communist International:

". . . To lead the masses to revolutionary positions in such a manner that the masses may, by their own experience, convince themselves of the correctness of the Party line."

We have always said and we repeat it today: He who does not understand this is a bad Communist, an enemy of organizational unity is he who hampers the unity of action of the working class in the daily struggle against the class enemy, against capitalism.

It is no accident that Otto Bauer does not raise the question of unity of action but the problem of the re-unification of Austrian Social-Democracy, which has been not so much routed as scrapped. An idea of what this re-unification would be like may be obtained from the fact that he cannot find even words of moral indignation against those "who by their conduct in the February struggles and afterwards have lost the confidence of the comrades," but he discovers the enemy once again on the Left Wing, about which he writes:

"It is therefore greatly to be feared that the Communist Party of Austria, upon instructions from its International, is repeating the old maneuver of speaking very eagerly about unity and the united front, but that it will pursue the end of preventing re-unification of the whole revolutionary proletariat of Austria in ONE Party."

What Otto Bauer says is in gross contradiction to the obvious truth. Both the Communist International and the Communist Party of Austria are eager — not in words but in deeds — that the Austrian labor movement should be united. They want one trade union movement, the continuation of the free trade unions as a single trade union movement, their transformation into organs of the class struggle, the continuation of the Schutzbund as the common organ of struggle of the whole revolutionary proletariat of Austria; they want one party, to lead the forces of the whole Austrian proletariat and of all toiling and exploited sections of the population for the overthrow of the fascist dictatorship, of capitalism, for the setting up of the proletarian dictatorship of Soviet power. The Communist Party of Austria has already rallied around itself many of the most active fighters of the anti-fascist proletarian revolution in Austria. Its doors stand open to all who want to fight this battle to the end. However, Otto Bauer's main worry is to construe a contradiction between the Communists, who were already on the right path before the February struggles, and those who took this path during the February struggles on the basis of their expariences with Social-Democracy. Where is this new argument of Otto Bauer's on the unity of the labor movement designed to lead us?

To put it shortly: To maintaining the split in the Austrian labor movement, to splitting it afresh. The Austrian working class is striving for unity — not on the basis of the Linz program, where, instead of the struggle for the dictatorship of the proletariat, the threat of proletarian dictatorship was included in the program. It does not seek union on the basis of a program of a former epoch which was then, in the time of Hainfeld, a great step forward, but which today cannot show it the path and the goal. The Austrian workers are looking not backward, but forward. Otto Bauer is once again working for a split in order to keep open the way to union with those who deservedly lost the confidence of the working class after the February days. The union which Otto Bauer proposes thus denotes the re-establishment of class collaboration with the Austrian bourgeoisie.

What sort of unity is required in the labor movement?

Unity of action is needed in every country, unity of action which unites the forces of the working class — no matter to what party or organization the workers may belong — for direct struggle against fascism in Germany, Austria and in all countries, unity of action which rallies them together for the defense of their interests against the offensive of capital. A unity of action which mobilizes the working class against the bourgeoisie, which gives the working class strength to lead the middle strata in town and country into the struggle against the bourgeoisie side by side with the proletariat.

Such unity of action opens the way to overcoming the split in the labor movement.

Theses on Soviet Power in the East

Chairman: I declare the sixth session of the Congress of the Peoples of the East open. Today we have on the agenda the question of Soviet construction in the East. Translation, please. [*Translation.*]

Accordingly, we shall proceed to hear the report on this question. I call on Comrade Bela Kun. [*Applause.*]

Bela Kun: Comrades, in support of theses which have been discussed in detail by the Presidium and which it now unanimously puts before you, I propose to address you as follows.

Mighty Tsarist Russia, an immediate neighbour of the peoples of the East, fell beneath the blows of the workers and the poorest peasants. This revolution did not stop half-way. It did not leave state power in the hands of those classes which more or less disliked the Tsarist regime but whose whole existence was based on oppression of the working people. This revolution did not leave intact the former structure of government, but smashed it, in order to build upon its ruins the authority of the workers and the poorest peasants, endeavouring by means of this authority to carry the struggle forward until no possibility of any sort of oppression was left. In another sense, too, this revolution did not stop half-way: it was not checked at the frontiers of the state, but, like a devouring flame, spread both westward and eastward. This spreading of the revolution to West and East threatens to bring about the final downfall of that system which, not content with exploiting the working people of its own countries, has come to flower in imperialist colonial policy and borne fruit in world war. A revolution in the West and in the East must inevitably follow upon the social revolution of the workers and poorest peasants of Russia. These two revolutions are organically interconnected not only because they are directed against a common foe, world imperialism, but also because the necessary premise of their victory is common, concerted struggle. In order to subjugate the colonial peoples the imperialist exploiters have mobilised the European workers, whom they have tried to win over to their side by means of bribes — crumbs from the super-profits extorted from the colonial peoples. This happened both in Britain and in Germany. They aimed in this way to deflect the workers from the path to revolutionary understanding. On the other hand, the imperialist bourgeoisie have given much thought, especially in recent times, to using against the European workers' movements the colonial troops they have recruited, exploiting the lack of consciousness of these soldiers so as to defend their shaken state power against the working class.

I, comrades, have had the opportunity to witness personally this sort of policy on the part of the imperialist bourgeoisie. When we, the workers and poorest peasants of Hungary, seized power, the French bourgeoisie at once attempted to strangle our revolution, using the hands of Moslem colonial troops. However, despite our difficulty in communicating with these soldiers owing to the difference of language, we nevertheless managed to find a way to their minds and hearts, and they threw down their arms when they were called upon to drown our revolution in blood.

The imperialist bourgeoisie usually succeeds in finding in the colonial countries a stratum of the native population, and in the semicolonial countries a ruling class, whose aid it can utilise so as to make its exploiting policy less difficult and less expensive than it would otherwise be, and also less costly in blood. The sultans and emirs and the ruling strata associated with them in the Eastern countries, after their own resistance has been broken, have always readily agreed to become collectors of tribute for the imperialist oppressors: thus, the Shah of Persia agreed to act as tribute-collector for Russian imperialism and for British imperialism, turn and turn about.

The Young Turks skinned the Turkish peasants on behalf of the German imperialists, and now the Anglophiles headed by the Sultan are depriving the Turkish peasant of his last cow in the interests of the Anglo-French imperialist bloc. The Emir Feisal, who is on the payroll of the French bankers, has agreed to break up the unity of the Turkish people and to make the Turkish peasantry accept the position of beasts of burden to the French imperialists.

The imperialist bourgeoisie found allies in the colonial and semicolonial countries of the East sooner than the revolutionary proletariat did. It helped these allies not only by giving them miserable crumbs from what it had plundered from the toiling poor of these countries, but also by training them in those methods by which it had deceived and stupefied its own working class.

Capitalism succeeded in holding in submission the rebellious worker masses of Europe only by persuading them that they too shared in state power, though this was in fact merely an instrument in the hands of the ruling class with which to oppress the working people. Similar to this was the parliamentary constitution in Turkey, drafted in accordance with the European pattern: although to the outward view it gave rights to the working people, in reality everything remained as before — domination by the pashas, tyranny of the officials, and no hindrance to the activity of the usurers who brought ruin upon the people.

The revolution of the European and American proletariat and poorest peasantry is directed precisely against those lies which aim to keep exploitation and oppression in being behind a screen of democracy, freedom and equality. The revolution of the Russian workers and poorest peasants created that form of government which puts power into the hands of the working masses not merely in words but also in deeds. This form is the Soviets of workers and peasants. Until the Russian workers and peasants took power through their Soviets the land remained in the hands of the landlords and the factories and mines in those of the capitalists. 'Freedom' merely gave the bourgeoisie freedom to squeeze sweat out of their workers and to refuse to the non-Russian nationalities the right to decide for themselves whether they wanted to remain within the Russian state or to be independent of it. The Communist revolution and the victory of the Soviet order at once transferred to the working people the land, factories and mines and, in place of the inequality between exploiters and exploited, established the equality of all working people. With the ending of exploitation there ended all interest in enslaving and exploiting other peoples. One of the first steps taken by the Soviet republic was recognition of the right to self-determination for all peoples and liberation of Russia's colonies. just as the Tsarist regime had secured alliances with the shahs and emirs, that is, with the ruling strata of the oppressed countries, so Soviet Russia immediately proposed an alliance to those toilers whom the old Russia, both Tsarist and democratic, had kept in a colonial situation.

Only the Soviet system made it possible to transfer power to those whose interest it was that the instruments of production should not serve the interests of a tiny handful of persons but should belong to all the working people.

The Soviets, these fighting organs of the workers and peasants, organs of their authority and government, are a new form of state. The workers and poorest peasants, having disarmed the enemies of the people, organise themselves in Soviets, take up arms, and themselves promulgate laws and decide what shall be the norms of the social order. The toiling masses themselves, either directly or through their representatives, pass the laws.

No parasites or exploiters boss the workers about, no usurers lord it over the poor. All these elements have been deprived of all rights. Soviet power is in sharp contrast to what prevails in the East today. It means rule by the toilers and the poor peasants, in place of rule by the rich and the parasites. I think that there is no delegate present here who is not convinced that oppression and exploitation can be ended only by introducing this form of state power. It is clear that until now, while our beys, khans, usurers and tribute-collectors possessed political rights, while they were able to distort the truth by means of all sorts of tricks and deceptions, to interpret the law in accordance with their own interests, and to resort to force of arms whenever their cunning did not help them — until now it has been quite futile to talk of putting an end to oppression and exploitation.

The theses I am laying before you set out in brief outline the essential features of Soviet power. Soviet power is not a system which cannot be adapted to the special conditions of a particular people or a particular region. In places where the predominant element consists of industrial workers, where exploitation is carried on by factory-owners and bankers, the Soviet organisation will be quite different from what it will be in places where the main part of the population is engaged in agriculture and where exploitation takes the form of usury. Whereas in Western states it is the factory-owners, bankers and big landowners who have, first and foremost, to be removed from power and stripped of rights, in the Eastern countries Soviet power must be directed, first and foremost, against usurers, kulaks, khans, beys, foreign exploiters and officials. The Eastern Soviets must, of course, be soviets of the peasant poor, and just as in Daghestan and Azerbaidzhan a method has been found for determining at what number of cattle the exploitation of others' labour begins, so in all other tribal communities it will be possible to determine rules which will ensure that Soviets so organised will really be organs of the toiling poor.

The hangers-on of the bourgeoisie know how to spread all manner of dreadful stories about the Soviet order. Those in the East who are interested in keeping the toilers of the East in slavery, either along with the Western capitalists or independently of them, have quickly learned to do the same.

Whereas, in the West, Soviet power is the expression of the dictatorship of the proletariat, in the East, in those countries where there is no industrial working class, it will be the expression of the dictatorship of the poorest peasantry. It is self-evident that where a factory exists, where there are, even if only in small numbers, some better educated and experienced industrial workers, these workers will be the leaders of the rural poor. They will not, of course, be leaders of the same sort as the previous rulers, who, concerned with their own well-being, led the poor peasants into exploitation and want, but will be leaders who, since they are themselves interested in the ending of all forms of oppression and exploitation, will act in the interests of the general good of the people.

Very briefly, I want to speak against the time-hardened view by which peoples who have not passed through a phase of capitalist development, and so through bourgeois democracy, have to experience all this before they can go over to the Soviet system. This idea is maintained for the sole purpose of keeping the poorest peasantry of the East for a still longer period in the power of the emirs, pashas, beys and foreign colonialists. There is another objection which is advanced against the formation of Soviets in the East, namely, that the dictatorship of the proletariat is impossible without an industrial proletariat, and in the East the numbers of the industrial proletariat are infinitesimal. To this we reply: 'In the West, Soviet power is indeed the form and expression of the dictatorship of the proletariat, but in the East, where the exploited element is not the industrial workers but the poorest peasantry, the latter must also be the leading element in the Soviets.'

There is yet another objection. 'The peoples of the East are not yet mature enough to decide their fate for themselves; they need to pass through the phase of bourgeois democracy in order to acquire the capacity for self-government.' Only imperialist colonialists argue like this.

In the language of the people it means: 'Wait, Moslem

poor peasants, until the pashas, beys, speculators and usurers deign to teach you how to take the land and power away from them.'

I think the falsity of this is clear to all the delegates. The Moslem poor have lived for many centuries under the rule of the Sultans, pashas and so on, and then came the colonialist merchants, those oppressors: they not only did not teach the people anything, but tried to keep them in ignorance. If the people are to wait, they will wait for centuries, until these hangmen have not only plundered them but have made them quite incapable of taking power for themselves. The ability to rule, like the ability to use a weapon, demands that you make a start and get some practice in: he who never handles a rifle will never learn to shoot.

In conclusion, I want to remind you of the changes which will be brought about in the pattern of everyday life, for the peoples of both East and West, by the common victory of their revolution. Economic intercourse between West and East will certainly not cease with the victory of the revolution. On the contrary, these ties will be very much closer than before; but they will be of quite a different kind from what they are today. The East is now united with the West by bonds of oppression and the coercion exercised by colonial troops. The means of colonial rule have always been alcohol, syphilis and weapons. Officers of the British and French imperialist armies have undressed the womenfolk of the oppressed Moslems not only with their eyes. The natural resources of the fertile Eastern lands have flowed away to the West — not into the hands of the Western workers, however, but into the coffers of the Western bankers, factory-owners and landlords.

These bankers and factory-owners, the oppressors of the Western workers, have always found allies in the East. The usurer who collects the fruits of Eastern fields, the state ruler and his entourage who have obtained loans from Western capitalists and ruthlessly collect the interest on these loans from the working peoples, these have always served as tools of colonial policy.

When the revolution of the proletariat and the poorest peasantry deprives the capitalists, landlords, factory-owners and bankers of all power and sends their myrmidons — generals, officials, priests — to the devil, and when power passes to the Soviets, which represent the masses of the working people, these new workers' and peasants' states will not, of course, pursue any aggressive aims in the East. They will not seek their allies among the Sultans and emirs, among the pashas and beys, and will not allow usurers to act as intermediaries in the economic dealings that will take place between the West and the peasantry of the East. The workers of the West and the peasants of the East can regulate their economic relations only directly, through their Soviet states. The Soviet state of the workers can sell the fruits of its labour only directly to the peasants of the East, and will never consent, can never consent, to receive goods produced by the stubborn labour of Eastern peasants through the mediation of usurers who rob them. Soviet states cannot follow the example of the capitalist system, which is entirely based upon buying and selling. Fraternal aid one to another, a just distribution of the fruits of joint labour — this is what can serve as the fundamental principle in the economic relations linking West and East after the victory of the revolution. And when the Soviet system triumphs in the West and the East there will disappear that difference which has existed and exists today between colonial and metropolitan countries. Entry into an international federation, into a world union of Soviet states, will equalise, so to speak, the East with the West, and will organically rule out any possibility of exploitation of the Eastern peoples.

Whoever appreciates that the liberating revolution of the peoples of the East, like the social revolution, will lead on to socialism cannot have any view on the question of the state system to be proposed for the East other than advocacy of Soviet power. In the days when bourgeois revolutions and the bourgeois order were flourishing, endeavours by the ruling strata of the East to establish a parliamentary system for the East as well, fully corresponding to capitalism and bourgeois democracy, were quite comprehensible. Establishing a parliamentary system meant at that time trying to raise the East to the level of the West, to give economic forces the opportunity to develop freely. Strictly speaking, the idea was that the working people should allow to sit astride their necks, instead of the foreign exploiters and oppressors, the native variety of the same breed.

At the present stage of development of the international revolution it is no longer a question of who will be the oppressors, among whom and in what way the wealth created by the toiling people is to be divided up. The Soviet system means an end to all forms of exploitation. The point is that the fruits of the toilers' labour are to be enjoyed by the toilers alone.

'Whoever does not work shall not eat.' Naturally, whoever wants to see the complete emancipation of the toilers of the East cannot be for a system which seeks, by means of its organs of power, to maintain exploitation. Whoever wants the peoples of the East to be freed from all forms of exploitation and oppression, whoever wants to be liberated from foreign colonialists and from the native agents of foreign imperialists, whoever wants to replace the rule of the pashas, khans, beys, usurers and other bloodsuckers by the rule of the working masses, can take no road but that of Soviet power. Whoever wants the poor peasants to cease being subject to the tyranny of the rich and their hangers-on, whoever wants the poor to be able to settle their affairs for themselves, will, on his return from the congress to his *aul,* to his village, fight tirelessly for that peasant agrarian revolution which is being realised in the East by Soviet power and which will lead the East out of its present oppressed situation. We are sure that at the Second Congress of the Peoples of the East the representatives of the federation of Eastern Soviet states will report on how the poor of the East took power, how they are building their Soviet organs, and how they are marching onward along the road which leads to the abolition of all exploitation — to communism. I propose the adoption of the following theses.

Theses on Soviet power in the East

1. The revolution of the peoples of the East against external and internal oppression, against the foreign imperialists and the local exploiters, puts on the agenda the question of the state system in all the countries of the East. The European bourgeoisie has succeeded for a long time, by means of all sorts of intrigues, in concealing from the propertyless and those with little property, the proletarian and semi-proletarian elements, the essential nature of state power as an instrument of oppression. In contrast to this, in the states of the East the coercive nature of the ruling power is quite obvious.

The lives and all the products of the labour of the poor, who are totally without political rights, are liable to be bought and sold by various sultans, shahs, emirs and tribal leaders, and by the rich and the bureaucratic cliques associated with them. This situation prepared the way for the imperialist exploiters, who, in the colonial countries and those reduced to a semi-colonial condition, always concluded their deals with the help of the state rulers and the higher officers and officials, at the expense of the poor.

2. As in Western states, the rich exploiting strata of the population in the Near-Eastern countries have tried to give their rule an appearance of democracy. The parliamentarising of Turkey and Persia and the transformation into democratic republics of Georgia (under the leadership of the Mensheviks), Armenia (under the leadership of the Dashnaks) and Azerbaidzhan (under the leadership of the Musavatists) took place under the slogans of freedom and equality. All these policies proved useless, however, even for creating a facade of democracy. Unheard-of poverty of the masses continues, together with prosperity for the agents of the foreign

imperialists. The land remains in the power of its previous owners, the old tribute system continues, bringing immeasurable harm to the working people, and not only is usury tolerated, it is backed by the state power, to the detriment of the poor. All this has revealed the falsity of the slogans about equality put forward by the Turkish, Persian and Azerbaidzhanian national-democratic parties, and also by the Menshevik and Dashnak parties, which operate under cover of socialist slogans.

3. The revolution of the toiling masses of the East will not come to a halt even after the rule of the foreign imperialists has been eliminated. It will not cease with a system which, under the false slogan of democracy, under cover of slogans of equality, seeks to maintain the power of the sultans, shahs, emirs, pashas and beys, seeks to maintain the oppression of the working people, inequality between the haves and the have-nots, the oppressors and the oppressed, between rich and poor, those who pay tribute and those who live on this tribute. The revolution will not halt at the estate boundaries of the landlords, proclaimed to be sacred: the Eastern peasantry, like the Russian, will develop their revolution to the dimensions of a huge agrarian peasant revolution, as a result of which the land must pass into the posse of the working people and all exploitation must disappear. just as the Russian peasantry carried through their agrarian revolution with the support of the industrial workers under the leadership of the Communist Party, and, welded together in Soviets, are now defending the land they took from the landlords and the power they took from the exploiters — in the same way the oppressed peasantry of the East will in their revolutionary struggle count upon the support of the revolutionary workers of the West, on the support of the Communist International and on that of the present and future Soviet states.

4. Soviet power and Soviet organisation are not only the instrument of power and the organisational form of the industrial proletariat, but also constitute the only appropriate

system whereby the working masses, after excluding from power the privileged, and consequently hostile, elements (landlords, speculators, higher officials, officers) can themselves build their own destiny. Only Soviet power gives power exclusively to the toiling poor. Unity of the Soviets, and their federation, is the only way to secure peaceful co-operation between the toiling elements of different peoples who have hitherto slaughtered each other in the East, and to help them to join forces to destroy the power of their oppressors, both foreign and native, and repel the oppressors' attempts to restore the former position.

5. So-called democratic self-government, putting the administration exclusively into the hands of the privileged strata (khans, beys, and so on) prevents the toiling masses from managing their own affairs. It deprives them of the possibility of learning to govern, stops them from acquiring the knowledge they need for this purpose. In contrast to this, experience among the peasants of Soviet Russia, Siberia, the Bashkir-Kirghiz republic and Turkestan has shown that the peasants of the Eastern countries are capable of managing their own affairs.

6. The victory of the Communist Party in the West will put an end to the exploitation of the Eastern peoples. But victory for the Communist revolution in the West will not mean that East and West can then get on without mutual economic links. On the contrary, the victory of the revolution in the East and in the West will mean that in relations between different countries there will be, instead of exploitation, reciprocal support and aid. After the victory of the Communist revolution, economic intercourse will take place between states, and so the economic intercourse of those Eastern states which have not adopted the Soviet system would only serve the interests of the small group of capitalists who, having obtained corn and raw materials, would carry on trade with the Western Soviet states in exactly the same way as they do at the present time with the imperialist states exploiting for this purpose the toiling masses of the East.

In the interests of complete liberation from imperialist exploitation, with transfer of the land to the toilers and emancipation from the power of speculator — exploiters, what is needed is removal from power of the non-working element, of all foreign colonialist elements (generals, officials, etc.) and of all privileged persons, and it is also necessary to organise the rule of the poor on Soviet principles. And all the other interests of the working people demonstrate to the East that it is imperative to establish Soviet power.

Chairman: Comrades, we now come to the vote on Comrade Bela Kun's theses, which were unanimously approved by the Presidium. Will those in favour please raise their hands. Who is against? Nobody. The theses are adopted. [*Applause.*] Let us proceed to the next question. Comrade Skachko will give the report on the agrarian question.

Skachko: Comrades, all the Eastern countries are peasant countries. Owing to various conditions, and principally to the oppressed state in which they have been kept by the Western European capitalists, who denied them the possibility of independent development, the inhabitants of these countries have not developed their own industry and to this day they are still exclusively engaged in agricultural labour. The great mass of the entire population of the Eastern countries consists of peasants. Emancipation of the peoples of the East means emancipation of the peasants. While in the Western countries the productive class consists mainly of industrial workers, and while it is the industrial proletariat that can be called the King of the West, in the Eastern countries the sole producers of material values are the peasants. And so only they can be called the Kings of the East, and the Eastern countries should belong only to them. Let us look, comrades, at how these Kings of the East live, these men and women whose labour sustains not only all the peoples of the East but also a good part of those of the

West. They live in the same wretched, pitiful, downtrodden and oppressed condition in which the peasantry of Western Europe lived many centuries ago. Though creating everything, they themselves enjoy none of it, and they bear the burden of unlimited oppression both by foreign capitalist conquerors and by their own privileged classes and despots. Various sultans, shahs, khans and beys, the masters of Eastern countries and lands, wallow in fabulous Eastern luxury while the peasants whose labour created this are dying of hunger and want, and are forced to leave their own very rich and fertile countries for alien lands, in search of the crust of bread they cannot obtain at home. Despite the fact that at the basis of the Moslem religion lay principles of religious communism, by which no man may be slave to another and not a single piece of land may be privately owned, and all religious institutions must make it their principal concern to care for the orphaned and indigent, nevertheless these religious principles have not saved the peasants from being reduced to serfdom, or preserved the land from seizure by landlords and despots. Gradually, these principles have been modified to the advantage of the ruling classes. The land, free and belonging only to God, was first declared to belong to the ruling Sultans and Shahs, and then became the property of feudalists and capitalists. The *waqf* lands which were given to the mosques and the clergy so that the income from them might support charitable institutions of value to the people, gradually lost their original function and became lands belonging to the clergy and to private persons, and the income from them, instead of being used for the benefit of the poor, was taken by the secular and ecclesiastical rulers — parasites who used these lands merely in order to exploit the poor peasants. The peasant, a free man according to the *shariat* was gradually turned into a slave, either by direct coercion on the part of the khans and beys or by economic compulsion based on the seizure of the land by the landlords. The situation of the peasantry of the Eastern peoples has not improved but constantly deteriorated, and has finally become so impossible and unbearable that no other way out is left for them but either to die a slow death from hunger or to break their servile chains and make a new life for themselves through social revolution.

How, indeed, can a man live in the conditions in which the Eastern peasant is living? Can we call a human life the existence that the wretched Persian *rayat* drags out? He is not a human being, he is only the beast of burden of his landlord, the *molkadar*. This landlord has power to dispose of his life and property, to execute him or to punish him with strokes of the cane, to take the peasant's wives and daughters for his harem. Comrades, all this is going on a few hundred versts from Baku, over which flies the red flag of the Workers' and Peasants' Socialist Republic. A few hundred versts from this place, where the peasants have taken power into their own hands, other peasants are living in a state of utter slavery. The Persian peasant cannot call a single fragment of land his own: he can easily be evicted by his landlord even from his farmhouse, to die of hunger in the barren steppe. For the right to work his land, for the right to grow corn, he has to hand over to the landlord four-fifths of the crop, four-fifths of what he has produced by the labour of his hands. Of all that he gets from the land by his own work he is allowed to keep only miserable leavings, while the main part is devoured by the various parasites who sit astride his neck and make his life a sheer unbearable torment of grim slavery.

That is how things are in Persia. But the position of the peasants is no better in the other countries of the East. Even in the most advanced of the Moslem countries, Turkey, the peasant is poverty-stricken. Although serfdom has been abolished in Turkey, nevertheless even there the peasant is being reduced to a servile situation through economic conditions. The despotic government of Turkey, which always looked upon the peoples subject to its rule as conquered peoples, always pursued one aim and one alone in its administration: to extract from the population as much income as possible, taking no account at all of what it cost the population to produce this income and what frightful want was created by this barbarous, ruthless extortion.

For centuries the despotic government of Turkey and its minions enforced such a frightful system of taxation and such a barbarous system of levying them, by means of tax-farming, that it completely ruined the peasantry and rendered them quite incapable of cultivating their holdings. In Turkey there are huge tracts of land, located in the most fertile vilayets, which are lying uncultivated, in utter desolation, the peasants having left the country, in search of a bite to eat. This has happened because the peasants are unable to work the abandoned land, since they have neither oxen, nor money, nor seed — they have none of the things they need in order to cultivate the land. In the southern part of Asia Minor, where also there are huge uncultivated tracts, there are more than 100,000 so-called marabas, nomadic wage-labourers who, having neither land, nor farmsteads, nor shelter, wander in hordes all over the country, looking for miserably-paid seasonal work on the landlords' estates. Even those peasants who still have a holding of their own cultivate it not for themselves but for all manner of usurers, to whom their indebtedness obliges them to hand over four-fifths of their crop. The extent of the exploitation and the poverty-stricken situation of the Turkish peasants is shown by statistics. These figures reveal that even in peacetime the Turkish peasant never has left, out of all the corn he produces, more than six poods per year per head, or three-quarters of a pound a day. Today the Russian proletariat, ruined by many years of war and receiving, in the big centres which are worst stricken with famine, only one-and-a-half pounds of bread a day, is better supplied with bread than the Turkish peasant living in a fertile country abounding in free land! In Turkey as in Persia the position of the peasant is absolutely unbearable. It is a position of utter want, chronic hunger, endless indebtedness and work for the tribute-collectors and usurers, without any certainty regarding his title to the land and with no hope whatsoever of any improvement in his wretched situation.

This is the desperate, oppressive situation in which the peasants of other Eastern countries also find themselves. Not to speak of the Armenians, driven from their land, forced to take refuge in barren mountains, deprived of their homes and livelihoods and stripped of all they possess by the Kurdish landlords, the aghas, the peasants of all the other nationalities, even if not driven from their land, have little joy in their lives, for they work not for themselves but for their oppressors. In Khiva, Bukhara and Afghanistan, where agriculture can be carried on only on irrigated land, all such land has been grabbed by the landlords, the beys and khans, and the peasants are able to work it only as wage-labourers. In India the British rulers have taken nearly all the land, and, seeking to squeeze the maximum revenue from this unfortunate country, have leased it out to big capitalists, so that the peasant can gain access to the land only as a sub-tenant or a wage-labourer. Out of what the Indian peasant produces from the land he has to hand over the lion's share to the British rulers and another share to the capitalist farmer, keeping for himself only such a share as enables him to die of hunger amidst the flowering valleys of his fertile homeland, his wondrous country with its countless riches.

Everywhere, in all the countries of the East, the peasantry, who alone create all the material values which sustain their own people and others as well, themselves drag out the wretched existence of downtrodden, starving slaves. Everywhere in the countries of the East the peasant, that king and creator of riches, is starving to death and groaning beneath the whips of his own and foreign oppressors. 'Starving to death', comrades, is no mere phrase: the peasantry of the East really are starving — it has been proved statistically. In order to escape from his miserable situation, to escape from want, poverty and hunger, the peasant of the Eastern countries must throw off the centuries-old oppression both of the foreign capitalist exploiters and of his own oppressors the sultans, khans, shahs and beys. [*Applause.*] The peasantry of the East have starved long enough, they have served their various oppressors long enough — now they must free themselves and

213

become the actual owners of their own land and the absolute masters of their fate. The many-millioned masses of peasants of the East must now rise up in all their colossal might and throw off all their oppressors, must take power into their own hands [*Applause*] by forming their own peasant Soviet government, by forming revolutionary peasant Soviets. All the sources of the oppression of the peasants must be destroyed — first and foremost, the system of landlordship which enslaves the peasant. Whoever does not work shall not eat; whoever does not till the land shall not possess it! [*Applause.*] All the land belonging to the landlords and feudalists, shahs and khans must be taken from them and given to the peasants, without any purchase-price, without any compensation to the former owners. Together with the land, all the animals and farm implements belonging to the estates of the feudalists and landlords must be taken, for the peasant must receive not only land but also the possibility of working it, and for this purpose he must seize all the instruments of production and all the wealth that his landlord oppressors possessed. Since there are in the East, besides the landlords' land, also huge tracts of state-owned land which are used by various secular and ecclesiastical institutions, officials and clergy, this land too must be taken from the ruling privileged classes and turned over to the peasants. Comrades, there is no cause to fear because some of this land belongs to the clergy. Of course the latter, who have concentrated huge tracts of land in their possession, and exploited peasant labour on this land, declare that this land belongs to God and therefore is inviolable, and the peasant dares not reach out to take it, but, comrades, this is all lies and fraud! Even according to the shariat, the land can belong only to him who tills it, and not to the clergy who have grabbed it, like the mujtahids in Persia, who were the first to violate the fundamental law of the Moslem religion. They are not defenders of this religion but perverters of it. They are just such parasites and oppressors as the feudal landlords, except that they are also hypocrites who disguise their character as oppressors behind the white turban and the Holy Koran. This mask of sanctity must be torn from them,

214

comrades, and the land they own must likewise be wrested from them and given to the working peasantry. [*Applause.*] All the confused and complicated legislation of the countries of the East, disguising private ownership under various masks and restricting the right of the possessor of a holding to use it as he pleases, preventing the peasant from cultivating his land as he wishes, must be swept away. Every peasant must have the right to utilise his land as he chooses, ignoring all such prohibitions and restrictions. [*Applause.*] Instead of the complicated and confused land laws which serve to enslave the peasant, it is necessary to establish just one land law, consisting of a single article: all land belongs to the state, and the right to use it belongs only to whoever works it with his own labour. [*Applause.*] That must be the only land law, giving the land to the toilers, to the peasants, and casting out from the land all parasites, exploiters and slaveowners. [*Tumultuous applause.*]

Then, comrades, attention must be paid to that scourge of the peasants of all the countries of the East which beats sweat and blood out of them and devastates the peasants' holdings — that fearful burden of taxes which the peasantry of Turkey, Persia and India have borne for hundreds of years. There is no need to tell you what these taxes have meant, what a fearful burden they have laid upon the peasants, how they have taken the skin, the blood, the very life of the peasants by means of a venal, corrupt administration. You know how the tithe provided for in the shariat has been turned into three-quarters and four-fifths of the peasant's crop, and how these taxes have reduced the peasantry of the Eastern countries to utter poverty. This scourge of taxation and the tyranny of officials and administrators associated with it must be destroyed, all taxes must be cancelled. The peasants must be freed from exploitation not only by the landlords but also by the state. [*Applause.*] But as it is clear that no human organisation can exist without incurring certain expenses, the newly-formed Soviet Government of the peasants will also need to have a certain amount of revenue at its disposal, and so the peasants will have to give their government a certain portion of what they produce, which will be needed to support the urban workers, the state machine and the Red Army which defends the peasants' freedom. However, this levy, its amount and the actual way it is to be collected will be decided and put into effect not by venal, bloodsucking officials but by the peasants' Soviets. [*Applause.*] Relieved of taxes, the peasantry must also be relieved of debts. You know, comrades, how burdened with debt the Eastern peasant is; you know that he is always in debt to a neighbouring landlord, or to some kulak, trader or usurer; you know that without contracting loans the Eastern peasant cannot carry on cultivating his exhausted holding, and is therefore always up to his ears in debt. This indebtedness of the peasants makes them serfs to the usurers and obliges them to work, their whole lives through, for the enrichment of a moneylender. If the land were to be taken over, but the power of the old debts were left pressing upon the peasants. it would mean that the latter would have escaped from the claws of the landlords merely to fall into those of the usurers. This heavy yoke of debt which harnesses the peasantry to the old world of slavery must be left behind in that old world, and one of the first steps taken by the risen revolutionary peasantry must be a complete and categorical cancellation of all peasant debts whatsoever — to the state, to land banks, to landlords, to traders, to usurers. All the debt liabilities of the peasants must be declared invalid. The new revolutionary world must tell the old world of the usurers that the peasants of the Eastern countries no longer owe anyone so much as a kopeck. [*Applause.*]

I have mentioned these, comrades, as the 'first steps to be taken by the revolutionary peasants in the countries of the East. I have indicated the measures which the peasants will need to take at once. When you return home you will advise the peasants what they must do. They must annihilate their feudalists and landlords, overthrow the power of the despots who rule them, take power into the hands of peasant Soviets, take possession of all landlords' land, state-owned land and *waqf* land, with all the animals and implements belonging to those lands, share them out among the peasant poor, stop paying taxes, cancel debts, and thereby free the peasantry from all exploitation from any and every quarter.

Then. when the peasants of the East have succeeded in casting off the yoke of the foreign capitalists and of their own oppressors, when the peasants of the East have succeeded in forming Soviet republics, closely linked with the Soviet republics of the West — then, with the aid of the friendly republics of the industrial proletariat, it will be necessary to organise on a wide scale the supply to the peasants of all the means and instruments of production needed for agriculture, so that agriculture may flourish in the Eastern countries, so that the land in these countries, which is rich and abundant, and which was once the cradle of all mankind, may again bloom with splendid flowers and again bring forth all the wealth of former times, and even more. The furnishing of these supplies will be the concern of the governments of the Eastern Soviet republics and of the proletariat of the Soviet republics of the West.

As well as supplying the peasants with means of production, with machines of tremendous power such as the East has not yet seen, it will be necessary to teach the peasants how to use them collectively, for these machines, which are extremely productive, easing the peasants' labour tenfold, are not suitable for work on small holdings they are adapted only to large areas and entail the need for joint cultivation of the peasants' land, the need to merge scattered labour into joint, collective labour, properly organised and shared. Only such joint, collective, properly-organised labour can transform the convict labour of the cultivator into labour which is sufficiently easy and pleasant. And it is for you, comrades, to show the peasantry the need to go over from scattered labour to joint labour. It is for you to show that the way of life of separate little economic cells, separate households, has always meant for the peasants and will continue to mean for them, the disintegration which makes possible their enslavement and oppression. In order that the peasantry may become a mighty force, they must merge into the close, organised unity into which the proletariat of the industrial countries of the West has merged. In order to achieve this unification it will be necessary to bring the peasants together into tens and hundreds of organisations of all kinds, agricultural and handicraft producers' artels and cooperatives and consumers' co-operatives of every sort, supplying the peasantry with all the products of urban industry that they need. All these organisations will free the peasantry from commercial middlemen and enable them to exchange their products directly for the products of factory industry. All middlemen, all parasites will be swept away, and the toilers will not have to hand over to them the slightest share of what they produce.

To arrive at this complete liberation of the peasantry from all their oppressors and all the parasites who feed at their expense, the peasantry will have to wage a protracted struggle, and this not only against the foreign capitalist conquerors but also against their own sultans and shahs, against their own landlords and feudalists, against their own bourgeoisie. Today in many Eastern countries, in Turkey, Persia and India, the peasantry is marching arm in arm with its own bourgeoisie in the fight to win independence for their countries from the foreign imperialist enslavers. Ibis path is the right one. At present, all the efforts of the Eastern peasantry must be directed to throwing off the yoke of the foreign imperialists which weighs upon them, freeing their countries from the yoke of the West-European bourgeoisie, the capitalists of Britain and France.

But the peasantry of the Eastern countries must remember that their task will not be finished when this liberation has been gained, that if they stop there, if they rest content with expelling the foreign oppressors, they will not be liberated at all. Political independence with retention of the capitalist system will not in the least guarantee liberation for the peasantry. If the government of Mustafa Kema in Turkey, or liberal-national governments in Persia and India, were to expel the British and then make peace with Britain on the basis of political independence of the Eastern countries, but with retention of the capitalist system in these countries, all the politically-independent Eastern countries would remain dependent economically. Political independence would not save them from penetration by industrial capital, and, with this penetration, or with the formation of native industrial capital and the development of native industry on the basis of private ownership of the means of production, the peasantry would be obliged to undergo an agonising period of primitive capitalist accumulation, in which they would be finally ruined, driven from their land, and all turned into wage-labourers with no holdings of their own. And this peasantry transformed into workers would be driven by the bourgeoisie, either native or foreign, into its plantations, factories and mines and made to work there, at miserable wages, for the enrichment of the capitalists — they would find themselves in even worse enslavement to capital than they are today.

The peasantry of the Eastern countries must firmly keep in mind the fact that liberation merely from the yoke of the foreign conquerors will not bring them real freedom. They need to liberate themselves also from their own oppressors, their own despotic rulers, their own landlords, and their own bourgeoisie, and, after setting up their own peasants' Soviet power, in alliance with the Soviet republics of Europe, they need to fight against the bourgeoisie of the whole world, fight for the overthrow of capitalism in all countries, both East and West. So long as somewhere the capitalist system has escaped destruction, so long as the entire world has not been transformed into a great federation of free workers' and peasants' Soviet republics, in which there will be no place for any exploitation or oppression, so long will the peasantry of the East be unable to attain real liberation and so long will they not have ensured for themselves a free, human existence.

Only with the final victory of the social revolution, only with the final establishment of the Communist order throughout the world, will the peasantry of the Eastern countries secure genuine freedom, both political and economic, becoming able to work for themselves on their own land, enjoying all the produce of their own labour and giving nothing to any oppressors and exploiters.

Therefore, there is no road for the peasantry of the East but to go forward together with the revolutionary workers of the West, in close alliance with the Soviet republics the latter have created, into struggle against both the foreign capitalist conquerors and their own despots, landlords, bourgeois and other oppressors, waging this fight to the end, not retreating until the complete victory of the social revolution, the establishment of the Communist order, which alone can bring real liberation to all the peoples of both West and East and alone can destroy all forms of oppression of one people by another and all forms of exploitation of man by man. [*Applause.*]

Comrades, all that I have said is summed up in the brief theses which the Congress Presidium has adopted. They explain how our Congress sees the situation of the peasants in the East, and the roads to their liberation which it advocates.

Theses on the agrarian question

1. The peasantry of the countries of the East, being the sole productive class and sustaining by their labour not only the landlords but also the entire bourgeoisie and bureaucracy, are crushed beneath a burden of survivals of feudalism, relations of bondage, landlords' extortions and state taxes, and find themselves in an absolutely unbearable situation of utter ruin, chronic hunger, endless indebtedness and work for landlords, tribute-collectors and usurers. The oppression and exploitation of the peasants of the Eastern countries by the ruling authority, by foreign capitalists and by their own landlords have reached such limits that not only development but even more human existence has become impossible for the peasants. and have degraded them to the position of downtrodden and perpetually

hungry beasts of burden.

2. The sources of the oppression and exploitation of the peasants are:

a) the retention of feudal relations, which place the peasants in both personal and economic dependence upon the landlords;

b) the seizure of the land by the landlords, which enables them, owing to the inadequate availability of free land, to reduce the peasants to bondage and turn them, though legally free, into *de* facto serfs;

c) the seizure of the land by the ruling authority, which leases out considerable tracts to the privileged classes and the capitalists, thus giving the latter a monopoly of landownership and obliging the peasants to become sub-tenants and labourers, under very burdensome conditions; d) the unbearable burden of taxes and the predatory way these are levied, by the irresponsible bureaucratic organs of the despotic ruling power; e) the lack of personal security, anarchy, and systematic brigandage by half-savage nomad tribes, which are backed by the ruling authority in their attacks on the peasants; f) the extreme ruin of the peasants caused by all these conditions, resulting in their complete impoverishment, and the monstrous indebtedness of the cultivators, arising from this ruin, so that they fall into a state of absolute economic dependence on usurers and the object of their work becomes the unending repayment of loans and the interest on loans to various banks, landlords, kulaks and usurers; g) the peasants' complete lack, as a result of their ruin, of means and instruments of production — money, agricultural machinery, draught animals, seed-corn, etc. — which means that it becomes impossible for the peasants to work for themselves on their own land, even when free and accessible land is available to them.

3. In order to bring about liberation from the unbearable burden of oppression, exploitation and ruin and to create the

conditions necessary for them to work for themselves so as to satisfy all their needs and make further development possible, the peasants of the Eastern countries must:

a) remove the prime source of all their oppression and exploitation, the power of the foreign capitalist conquerors and of their own despotic tyrants, the sultans, shahs, khans and beys, with their entire parasitic train of bureaucrats and spongers, and take power, with all its administrative, economic and financial functions into their own hands, by forming local and central peasants' Soviets and setting up peasant Soviet republics of the East, linked in one indissoluble federation with the Soviet republics of the countries of the West;

b) refuse to fulfil any obligations towards the feudal landlords, overthrow their power, abolish all personal and economic dependence upon them, abolish large-scale landownership, under whatever legal form it may be concealed, take the land from the landlords without any purchase-price or compensation, and divide it among the peasants, tenants and labourers who till it, along with the land, take the herds of animals belonging to the landlords and divide them, in the first place among the labourers who possess no animals at all, and then among the tenants and poor peasant cultivators; turn over the implements found on the landlords' estates to collective ownership by the peasants who have occupied the land — the peasants should unite in groups, concentrating the implements made available to them for use in collective cultivation of the land, which ensures the best results and the most rapid development of the peasants' economy and of their prosperity;

c) take over all lands belonging to the state and to its various institutions, both secular and spiritual (including waqf lands) and divide them among the peasants and tenants, subtenants and labourers who work these lands, with complete abolition of all the rights of the big tenant-farmers who act as intermediaries between the state and the peasants, and confiscation for the benefit of the peasants of all the animals and implements belonging to these tenant-farmers;

d) cancel all existing land legislation and all restrictions on the right to use the land and to make changes on the surface of the holdings; proclaim that all land, regardless of its origin and independently of the rights of any owners or occupiers, belongs to the state and that it can be utilised free of charge by anyone who works it with his own labour; establish by means of a single land law the rule that 'whoever works a plot of land with his own labour is the possessor of that land and the owner of its produce,' and at the same time declare that the small-scale holdings of peasants who do not use others' labour are inviolable, and nobody has the right to encroach upon them for any purpose whatsoever;

e) regulate the utilisation of local irrigation water-supplies and irrigated land, this to be the responsibility of the peasant soviets, both local and central;

f) secure the interests of the nomadic tribes, assigning for their use areas of pasture-land sufficient to meet their needs, and at the same time take all measures required to ease the transition of the nomads to a settled way of life;

g) cancel all existing taxes, including the tithe, replacing them with a single assessed levy of a proportion of all the peasants' produce, this being necessary for the maintenance of the urban workers and of the army; the amount of this levy, its assessment and also the actual process of collection to be determined and implemented by the peasant Soviets, and everything taken from the peasants by means of this levy to be compensated by an assessed payment to the peasants of all the goods produced by urban industry which they need;

h) cancel all peasants' debts of every kind, to the state and to its various secular and spiritual institutions, to banks, landlords, and traders, and recognise as invalid all manner of peasants' debt liabilities;

i) undertake, after organising peasant soviets and

peasant soviet republics in the East, with the help and support of the Soviet republics of the industrial West, the supplying to the peasants, on an extensive scale, of agricultural machinery, tools, draught animals and other means of production needed for carrying on agriculture, arranging for joint use of these means of production by all the peasants; undertake the organising of agronomic aid to the peasants and collective working of the land, without any compulsion of individual cultivators to participate in this; undertake the organising of peasant producers' co-operatives, both for agriculture and for handicrafts, with extensive state support and gradual statisation; undertake the organising among the peasants of consumers' co-operatives with extensive state support and gradual statisation, arranging through these co-operatives the supply to the peasants of all the products of urban industry needed by them; organise on free, uncultivated land, in step with the supplying of the peasants with all the means of production needed for agriculture, Communist soviet farms, to be run, under state supervision, by agricultural workers organised in production associations; endeavour to develop these Communist soviet farms on as wide a scale as possible, with a view to using their surplus produce for exchange for needed urban-industrial goods which are produced by the industrial countries of Europe.

The mere establishment of the political independence of the Eastern countries , such as Turkey, Persia, Afghanistan, etc., as also the proclamation of the merely political independence of the colonial countries — India, Egypt, Mesopotamia, Arabia, etc. — cannot liberate the peasants of the East from oppression, exploitation and ruin. If the capitalist system is retained in Europe and Asia, the countries of the East which win freedom from political dependence upon the imperialist countries of the West, being more backward industrially, inevitably remain in complete economic dependence upon the latter, and, as before, serve as areas for the application of the finance-capital of the European industrial countries, which is associated with capitalist exploitation of the peasants and workers. If the capitalist system is retained, then, even in the event of the conquest of complete political independence by the countries and colonies of the East, the peasants of these countries must inevitably pass through an agonising period of primitive capitalist accumulation, associated with their final ruin, eviction from the land, proletarianisation and transformation into wage-earning factory hands or agricultural labourers, deprived of their own holdings and compelled to sell their labour-power. The peasantry of the East, now marching arm in arm with their own democratic bourgeoisie to win independence for their countries from the West-European imperialist powers, must remember that they have their own special tasks to perform, that their liberation will not be achieved merely by the winning of political independence, and that therefore they cannot halt and rest content when this is won. The peasantry of the East must go forward, continuing to fight even after the independence of their countries has been won — they must continue the fight against their dependence on their own landlords and their own bourgeoisie, who will certainly try, after the achievement of independence, to replace exploitation of the peasants by the West-European capitalists by exploitation of these peasants by themselves, the local landlords and bourgeoisie.

For complete and real liberation of the peasantry of the East from all forms of oppression, dependence and exploitation, what is further required is overthrow of the rule of their own landlords and bourgeoisie and the establishment in the countries of the East of the Soviet power of the workers and peasants. Only the complete abolition of the capitalist system, in West and East alike, will enable the peasants of the East not to lose but to retain and develop their holdings, and, avoiding the necessity of passing through an agonising phase of primitive capitalist accumulation, to advance, with the help of the working class of the more advanced countries, through a certain stage of development, to the Communist order, which will ensure for every peasant full freedom and full use of all the products of his labour.

Only the complete triumph of the social revolution and the establishment of a world-wide Communist economy can free the peasantry of the Eastern countries from ruin, want, poverty, famine, oppression and exploitation. And so for the peasants of the East, in their struggle for emancipation, there is no other road than that of struggle, together with the advanced revolutionary workers of the West, in close alliance with the Soviet republics these have formed, both against foreign capitalist conquerors and against their own despots — landlords, bourgeois and other oppressors: carrying on this struggle without retreating until complete victory has been won over the world bourgeoisie, until the complete victory of the social revolution, until the final establishment of the Communist order, which alone can bring true liberation to all the peoples of West and East alike, abolishing all oppression of one people by another and every kind of exploitation of man by man. [*Translation.*]

Chairman: I request the comrades to come over here so that we can take the vote. Comrades, we are going to vote on the resolution on Comrade Skachko's report. You have heard his report and his clear theses, which have been approved by the Presidium.

All in favour of the theses, please raise your hands. Anyone against? No-one. Adopted unanimously. [*Tumultuous applause. Shouts of* 'Bravo'.]

Please give me your attention. Tomorrow at 10 a meeting of the non-Party fraction will be held here. I request the non-Party delegates to be present in as large numbers as possible. Comrade Zinoviev will also be present.

Secretary: Comrades, the Communist fraction will meet tomorrow at 9 a.m. in the Red Army Club. Everyone is to attend. Important questions will be decided.

Chairman: Comrades, tomorrow at 5 p.m. we shall hold the last session of our Congress. It is understood that absolutely every delegate must be present at this last session.

www.ingramcontent.com/pod-product-compliance
Lightning Source LLC
Chambersburg PA
CBHW060246290526
45789CB00001B/213